I0446171

Money Mastery

Unlocking the Path to True Financial Freedom

TABLE OF CONTENTS

Copyright Page

© 2023 by Ravneet Singh. All rights reserved.

No part of this book may be reproduced, stored in a retrieval system, or transmitted in any form or by any means, electronic, mechanical, photocopying, recording, scanning, or otherwise, except as permitted under the Copyright Act, 1957, without the prior written permission of the publisher.

This book is protected under the copyright laws of India. Any reproduction or unauthorized use of the material or artwork contained herein is prohibited without the express written consent of the publisher.

This book is intended solely for informational and educational purposes. It should not be used as a substitute for professional, financial, or legal advice. The author and publisher make no representations or warranties of any kind, express or implied, about the book's completeness, accuracy, reliability, suitability, or availability or the information, products, services, or related graphics contained in the book for any purpose. Therefore, any reliance placed on such information is strictly at your own risk.

This book may include affiliate links. The author may receive a commission for purchases made through these links. However, the content or recommendations made in this book are acceptable. The author only includes affiliate links for products or services that they believe will add value to the reader.

Please consult with a professional advisor or attorney before making any financial decisions based on the content of this book. The author and publisher are not responsible for errors, inaccuracies, or omissions. They shall not be liable for any loss or damage of any kind, including, but not limited to, any direct, indirect, incidental, consequential, special, or exemplary damages arising from or in connection with the use of this book or its information.

Published by Ravneet Singh

Printed in India

Introduction

Welcome to the Journey

In this opening chapter, readers are invited to embark on a transformative journey towards true financial freedom. The introduction begins with a warm welcome, establishing a connection between the author and the reader. It briefly introduces the concept of financial freedom, emphasizing its multifaceted nature that goes beyond mere monetary gains.

To engage the reader, personal anecdotes or success stories related to financial mastery may be shared, creating a relatable and inspiring atmosphere. The purpose of this book is outlined — to guide readers in unlocking the path to true financial freedom through a comprehensive and holistic approach.

The introduction aims to pique the reader's curiosity, making them eager to explore the chapters that follow. It sets the stage for self-reflection and growth, inviting readers to consider their current relationship with money and the possibilities that lie ahead. Ultimately, this introduction serves as a motivational launchpad for the enriching journey towards financial mastery and a life of abundance.

Briefly introduce the concept of financial freedom

Financial freedom is a state of financial well-being where an individual has the ability to make life choices without being overly concerned about the financial impact of those decisions. It goes beyond simply having a high income and involves achieving a level of financial security and independence that allows for a fulfilling and comfortable lifestyle.

In the context of "Money Mastery: Unlocking the Path to True Financial Freedom," the concept is presented as a holistic approach to wealth. It encompasses not only the accumulation of assets and financial resources but also the development of a mindset and lifestyle that align with one's goals and values. True financial freedom involves mastering various aspects of personal finance, including budgeting, investing, debt management, and conscious spending, to create a sustainable and resilient financial foundation.

The journey to financial freedom is often characterized by strategic planning, disciplined financial habits, and a continuous commitment to learning and growing. It empowers individuals to pursue their passions, make choices based on personal values, and achieve a sense of security and contentment in their financial lives. Throughout the book, the reader will explore practical strategies and insights to unlock this path to true financial freedom, fostering a comprehensive understanding of wealth that extends beyond monetary measures.

Share personal experiences or success stories related to financial mastery

- **The Transformation of Sarah's Financial Landscape:**

  Imagine Sarah, a young professional burdened with student loans and credit card debt. Through disciplined budgeting and strategic debt repayment, Sarah managed to pay off her debts ahead of schedule. She then redirected those funds into smart investments, leveraging the power of compounding. Over time, Sarah not only achieved financial stability but also realized her dream of starting a side business, turning her passion into an additional income stream. Sarah's journey showcases the transformative power of mastering one's finances and the ripple effects it can have on various aspects of life.

- **James' Early Retirement Adventure:**

  Picture James, who diligently followed a plan of aggressive saving and investing throughout his career. By making informed investment decisions and living below his means, James accumulated a substantial nest egg. In his mid-forties, he made the bold decision to retire early and pursue a life of travel and personal fulfillment. James' story illustrates the concept of financial freedom as the ability to retire on one's terms and enjoy life without being tied to a traditional work schedule. His journey inspires others to consider alternative paths to retirement and prioritize life experiences over the conventional nine-to-five grind.

Defining True Financial Freedom

Financial freedom is a term often used, but its true essence extends far beyond the mere accumulation of wealth. In the context of this book, we delve into a comprehensive definition that encompasses various dimensions, creating a roadmap for readers to embark on a journey towards true financial freedom.

1. Beyond Monetary Measures:

True financial freedom extends beyond the size of your bank account. It's about achieving a state where you have the autonomy to make life choices based on your values and aspirations. While monetary wealth is a part of the equation, this definition emphasizes the holistic nature of financial freedom.

2. The Power of Choices:

At its core, financial freedom grants you the power of choice. It's the ability to pursue a career you love, invest time in meaningful relationships, and engage in experiences that bring joy. It's about breaking free from financial constraints that might limit your options and determining your path in life.

3. Security and Peace of Mind:

True financial freedom instils a sense of security and peace of mind. It involves building a robust financial foundation that can weather economic storms and unexpected challenges. It's the confidence that you have the resources to navigate life's uncertainties without compromising your well-being.

4. Time as a Valuable Asset:

Time is a finite resource, and achieving financial freedom means reclaiming control over your time. Whether it's early retirement, pursuing passion projects, or spending more time with loved ones, true financial freedom enables you to allocate your time in alignment with your priorities.

5. Lifelong Learning and Growth:

Financial freedom is a journey of continuous learning and growth. It's not just a destination but a process that evolves with changing circumstances. Embracing a mind of curiosity and adaptability allows you to navigate the complexities of personal finance and make informed decisions throughout your life.

6. Impact and Legacy:

Beyond personal gain, true financial freedom opens doors to make a positive impact on others and leave a lasting legacy. Whether through philanthropy, mentorship, or community involvement, it's about contributing to a greater good and shaping a legacy that extends beyond individual accomplishments.

In the chapters that follow, we will explore practical strategies and insights to help you achieve this multi-faceted definition of financial freedom. By understanding and integrating these principles into your life, you will be on the path to unlocking a future characterized by autonomy, choices, security, and the fulfillment of your deepest aspirations—Let's embark on this transformative journey together.

Clarify what financial freedom means

Financial freedom is a state of financial well-being and empowerment where an individual has the ability to make life choices without being unduly constrained by financial concerns. It goes beyond the simple accumulation of wealth and involves achieving a level of financial security and independence that enables a fulfilling and comfortable lifestyle.

Key aspects of what financial freedom means include:

Autonomy and Choice: Financial freedom provides the freedom to make choices based on personal values and goals. It allows individuals to pursue careers they are passionate about, engage in meaningful experiences, and allocate time according to their priorities.

Freedom from Debt: Achieving financial freedom often involves managing and eliminating debt. Being free from the burden of debt allows individuals to allocate more of their income toward building wealth and pursuing their desired lifestyle.

Savings and Investments: Financial freedom involves building a robust financial foundation through savings and strategic investments. This not only provides a safety net for unexpected expenses but also allows for wealth growth over time.

Security and Peace of Mind: True financial freedom brings a sense of security and peace of mind. Individuals feel confident in their ability to handle financial challenges, navigate economic downturns, and withstand unexpected events without compromising their well-being.

Time Freedom: Financial freedom enables individuals to have greater control over their time. Whether it's the flexibility to choose when and how to work or the option for early retirement, having control over one's time is a significant aspect of financial freedom.

Lifelong Learning and Adaptability: Financial freedom is a dynamic process that involves continuous learning and adaptation. It requires staying informed about financial matters, adapting to changes in economic conditions, and making informed decisions throughout different life stages.

Impact and Legacy: Beyond personal gain, financial freedom provides the opportunity to make a positive impact on others and leave a lasting legacy. This could involve philanthropy, supporting causes one is passionate about, and contributing to the well-being of the community.

In essence, financial freedom is a holistic and personalized concept that varies for each individual. It's about achieving a balance between financial security, the pursuit of personal goals, and the ability to contribute positively to the lives of others. Through intentional financial planning and mindful decision-making, individuals can strive to attain and maintain a state of true financial freedom.

Emphasise the holistic approach to wealth beyond monetary gains

Emphasizing the holistic approach to wealth beyond monetary gains is a fundamental aspect of understanding and achieving true financial freedom. This approach recognizes that wealth encompasses more than just financial assets; it extends to various dimensions of well-being, personal fulfillment, and overall life satisfaction.

1. Health and Well-being:

True wealth includes a focus on physical and mental well-being. A holistic approach to wealth acknowledges that good health is a priceless asset. Investing time and resources in maintaining a healthy lifestyle contributes significantly to one's overall wealth and quality of life.

2. Relationships and Community:

Building and nurturing meaningful relationships is an essential component of holistic wealth. True wealth involves strong connections with family, friends, and community. Investing in positive relationships contributes not only to emotional well-being but also to a support system that extends beyond financial matters.

3. Personal Development and Growth:

Holistic wealth considers the continuous pursuit of knowledge, personal development, and self-improvement. Investing in skills, education, and experiences that contribute to personal growth adds a profound dimension to one's wealth beyond financial assets.

4. Work-Life Balance:

Achieving wealth is not solely about accumulating financial resources at the expense of personal time and well-being. A holistic approach values a healthy work-life balance, ensuring that individuals have the time and freedom to enjoy life outside of professional commitments.

5. Purpose and Fulfillment:

True wealth is aligned with a sense of purpose and fulfillment. This involves pursuing activities, passions, and endeavors that bring joy and satisfaction. The holistic perspective acknowledges the importance of aligning one's financial goals with a large purpose in life.

6. Environmental and Social Responsibility:

Holistic wealth recognizes the impact of individual actions on the broader world. Considering environmental and social responsibility as part of wealth acknowledges the interconnectedness of individuals with their communities and the planet.

7. Emotional Intelligence and Well-being:

Emotional intelligence and well-being contribute significantly to holistic wealth. Understanding and managing emotions, cultivating resilience, and prioritizing mental health are integral components of a comprehensive approach to personal wealth.

By embracing this holistic perspective, individuals can redefine and expand their understanding of wealth. It encourages a balanced and sustainable approach to life that goes beyond the narrow focus on monetary gains. The pursuit of true financial freedom, within this context, becomes a journey towards a rich and fulfilling life that encompasses various facets of well-being and personal satisfaction.

Chapter 1:

Understanding Your Relationship with Money

In this foundational chapter, we explore your relationship with money. We begin by dissecting your money minds, unraveling the influences that shape your financial beliefs. Through self-reflection, you'll assess current financial habits and clarify aspirations. We tackle limiting beliefs, offering strategies for transformation. The chapter culminates in setting clear, actionable financial goals, providing the groundwork for your journey toward true financial freedom.

1.1 Exploring Your Money Mindset

Assessing and Reshaping Beliefs About Money

This critical section of our exploration delves into the intricate web of beliefs that often shape our relationship with money. By understanding the origin of these beliefs—whether influenced by cultural backgrounds, familial upbringing, or societal expectations—you gain profound insights into the forces guiding your financial decisions.

Practical exercises are designed to illuminate your subconscious beliefs about money, bringing them to the front of your awareness. We then embark on a journey of reassessment and challenge, encouraging you to question limiting beliefs that may hinder financial growth.

The aim is not only to identify these beliefs but also to provide actionable strategies for reshaping them.

As you engage in this process, you'll uncover the potential barriers preventing you from achieving financial success. Reshaping your beliefs becomes a transformative step towards fostering a positive and empowering financial mindset, setting the stage for a more intentional and prosperous financial future. In understanding and reshaping these beliefs, you empower yourself to navigate the path to true financial freedom with newfound clarity and purpose.

Identifying and overcoming limiting beliefs

In the pursuit of financial mastery, understanding and addressing limiting beliefs is a pivotal stage in reshaping your relationship with money. Limiting beliefs are often deeply ingrained convictions that hinder financial progress, stemming from influences such as upbringing, societal expectations, or past experiences. This section is dedicated to unravelling these beliefs, providing you with the tools and insights needed to overcome them.

Understanding the Roots:

To effectively tackle limiting beliefs, it's crucial first to identify their roots. Through self-reflection and introspection, you'll explore the origin of these beliefs and recognize their impact on your financial decisions. Whether it's a belief in scarcity, fear of failure, or notions of unworthiness, acknowledging these roots is the initial step toward dismantling their influence.

Challenging Assumptions:

Once identified, this section guides you in challenging these assumptions. It encourages a critical examination of the evidence supporting these limiting beliefs and prompts you to question their validity. By dismantling the logical underpinnings of these beliefs, you pave the way for a mindset shift towards abundance, possibility, and financial empowerment.

Strategies for Overcoming:

Practical strategies are then introduced to aid in overcoming limiting beliefs. From positive affirmations to visualization techniques, you'll have a toolkit at your disposal. Additionally, stories of individuals who successfully navigated similar challenges will inspire and provide real-world examples of triumph over limiting beliefs.

Cultivating Empowering Beliefs:

The ultimate goal is to replace limiting beliefs with empowering ones. Through intentional mind cultivation, you'll foster a positive outlook on your financial journey. This involves embracing beliefs that align with your goals, acknowledge your worth, and instilling confidence in your ability to achieve financial success.

As you progress through this section, envision it as a transformative process—a liberation from the constraints of limiting beliefs and a powerful stride towards a mindset conducive to financial abundance. By identifying and overcoming these barriers, you lay the foundation for a future defined by financial freedom and limitless possibilities.

1.2 Financial Self-Reflection

In the pursuit of financial mastery, introspection becomes a compass guiding your journey. This section, dedicated to financial self-reflection, invites you to a deliberate examination of your current financial landscape. It serves as a crucial checkpoint, allowing you to assess your financial habits, values, and aspirations.

Assessing Current Financial Habits:

Begin by objectively evaluating your existing financial habits. This includes an analysis of spending practices, saving practices, and investment choices. By gaining clarity on your present financial behaviours, you lay the groundwork for intentional and informed decision-making.

Clarifying Financial Values:

Understanding your values is fundamental to financial well-being. This section prompts you to identify the financial principles that matter most to you. Whether it's prioritizing experiences over possessions or emphasizing long-term security, clarifying your values provides a compass for aligning your financial decisions with your broader life goals.

Defining Financial Aspirations:

What are your financial aspirations? This segment encourages you to set clear, attainable goals. Whether it's eliminating debt, building an emergency fund, or embarking on an investment journey, articulating your aspirations creates a roadmap for your financial future.

Aligning Finances with Life Goals:

Financial well-being is not an end in itself but a means to achieve broader life objectives. Reflect on how your current financial situation aligns with your life goals. This connection helps you prioritize and allocate resources to areas that contribute most significantly to your overall well-being.

Creating a Foundation for Action:

Financial self-reflection is not an exercise in judgment but an opportunity for empowerment. By embracing the insights gained from this process, you create a foundation for informed and purpose-driven financial decisions. It positions you to navigate the upcoming chapters with a clear understanding of where you stand and where you aspire to be.

In essence, financial self-reflection is a mirror reflecting the current state of your financial affairs. It is a tool for empowerment, enabling you to make intentional choices that propel you towards true financial freedom. As you engage in this reflective journey, envision it as a stepping stone towards a future where your financial decisions align seamlessly with your life aspirations.

Evaluating current financial habits

Assessing and understanding your current financial habits is a pivotal step on your path to financial mastery. In this phase, we embark on a thorough examination of how you manage and allocate your financial resources. This process involves a detailed analysis of your spending patterns, saving practices, and investment decisions.

1. Spending Patterns:

Begin by scrutinising your day-to-day spending. Evaluate where your money goes, distinguishing between needs and wants. This assessment sheds light on potential areas for optimization and highlights spending habits that align with your financial goals.

2. Saving Practices:

Analyze your saving habits, considering both short-term and long-term goals. Assess the consistency of your saving efforts and the effectiveness of your chosen saving mechanisms. This step lays the foundation for building a robust financial safety net and working towards future aspirations.

3. Investment Decisions:

Evaluate your investment portfolio and decisions. Assess the alignment of your investments with your risk tolerance, financial goals, and time horizon. This critical analysis ensures that your investment strategy is conducive to long-term wealth growth.

4. Debt Management:

Examine your approach to debt, including outstanding loans and credit card balances. Assess the impact of interest rates and the feasibility of your debt repayment plan. This evaluation sets the stage for strategic debt management, a key element in achieving financial freedom.

5. Budgeting Effectiveness:

Reflect on the effectiveness of your budgeting practices. Determine if your budget is realistic, allowing for both necessary expenses and discretionary spending. This assessment serves as a practical tool for aligning your financial habits with your overarching financial objectives.

By engaging in this comprehensive evaluation of your current financial habits, you gain valuable insights into the dynamics of your financial decision-making. It positions you to make informed adjustments, cultivating habits that propel you towards financial success and the realization of your broader life goals.

Setting personal financial goals

Setting clear and achievable financial goals is a cornerstone of your journey toward financial mastery. In this crucial phase, we guide you through the process of articulating your aspirations and creating a roadmap that aligns your financial decisions with your broader life objectives.

1. Clarifying Short-Term Objectives:

Begin by identifying short-term financial goals. These could include building an emergency fund, paying off high-interest debt, or saving for a specific purchase. Clarity on short-term objectives allows for focus and tangible progress.

2. Defining Mid-Term Milestones:

Move on to defining mid-term financial milestones. These goals might encompass saving for a down payment on a home, funding education, or achieving a specific level of investment growth. This step ensures that your financial journey is strategically mapped for the medium term.

3. Articulating Long-Term Aspirations:

Consider your long-term financial aspirations, such as retirement planning, creating generational wealth, or achieving financial independence. Clearly articulating these long-term goals provides a guiding light for your financial decisions over the years.

4. Ensuring Specificity and Measurability:

Ensure that your goals are specific and measurable. Rather than a vague aspiration like "save more," articulate a concrete target, such as "save $5,000 in the next 12 months." This specificity enables you to track progress and celebrate achievements.

5. Aligning with Personal Values:

Your financial goals should align with your values and priorities. Reflect on what truly matters to you and structure your financial objectives accordingly. This alignment fosters a sense of purpose, making it more likely that you'll stay committed to your financial journey.

6. Prioritizing and Sequencing:

Prioritize your goals based on their significance and urgency. Sequencing your goals ensures a systematic approach, allowing you to focus on one objective at a time while maintaining a holistic view of your financial landscape.

7. Incorporating Flexibility:

Recognize that life is dynamic, and circumstances may change. Build flexibility into your goal-setting process to accommodate unexpected events or shifts in priorities. This adaptability ensures that your financial goals remain realistic and achievable.

By the end of this process, you will have a well-defined set of financial goals that serve as a guiding framework for your journey toward financial freedom. These goals will not only inform your day-to-day financial decisions but also inspire a sense of purpose and direction in your overall financial strategy.

Chapter 2:

Building a Solid Financial Foundation

In this pivotal chapter of "Money Mastery," we focus on constructing a resilient financial foundation. This entails practical steps to fortify your financial well-being. Beginning with the creation of an effective budget, we guide you through the process of allocating resources wisely, ensuring a balance between spending, saving, and investing. Emphasis is placed on the importance of emergency funds and strategic saving practices, laying the groundwork for financial security. Debt elimination strategies are explored to liberate your finances from burdensome liabilities.

Moving beyond basics, we delve into the power of compound interest and the principles of diversification and risk management in investment. The chapter culminates in an exploration of passive income streams and real estate opportunities as avenues for sustained financial growth. By the end, you will possess a robust financial framework, equipped with the knowledge and practices essential for enduring financial success and paving the way toward true financial freedom.

2.1 Creating a Budget That Works

Crafting an effective budget is a fundamental step toward financial mastery. This section guides you through the process of developing a budget that aligns with your financial goals and lifestyle.

1. Income Assessment:

Begin by thoroughly evaluating your sources of income. Understand your after-tax income and consider all revenue streams, including salaries, bonuses, and supplementary income.

2. Fixed and Variable Expenses:

Distinguish between fixed and variable expenses. Fixed costs, such as rent and utilities, remain constant, while variable expenses, like entertainment and dining out, fluctuate. Categorizing expenditures provides clarity and aids in budget allocation.

3. Prioritizing Financial Goals:

Align your budget with your financial objectives. Prioritize goals such as debt repayment, emergency fund creation, and savings for long-term aspirations. This step ensures that your budget serves as a strategic tool for achieving desired outcomes.

4. Allocating for Savings and Investments:

Devote a portion of your budget to savings and investments. Whether for short-term goals or long-term wealth building, consistent allocation toward savings is integral to financial stability and growth.

5. Contingency Planning:

Incorporate a contingency fund within your budget to address unforeseen expenses. This emergency fund acts as a financial safety net, providing peace of mind and resilience during unexpected financial challenges.

6. Regular Monitoring and Adjustments:

Regularly monitor your budget to assess its effectiveness. Be prepared to make adjustments as circumstances change. Flexibility in budgeting ensures adaptability to evolving financial needs and goals.

7. Tools and Resources:

Utilize budgeting tools and resources to streamline the process. Various apps and software platforms offer user-friendly interfaces for tracking income, expenses, and financial goals, enhancing the efficiency of your budgeting efforts.

Creating a budget that works is not just about restriction; it's a dynamic tool for financial empowerment. Through intentional budgeting, you gain control over your financial resources, fostering a disciplined approach that propels you toward your desired financial future.

Practical tips for budgeting success

Navigating the terrain of budgeting demands a strategic approach and practical insights. Here are detailed tips to ensure your budget not only works but becomes a powerful ally in your journey to financial mastery:

1. Comprehensive Expense Tracking:

Initiate your budget by meticulously tracking all expenses. From major bills to daily coffee runs, a comprehensive record unveils spending patterns, allowing for informed decision-making.

2. Categorize with Precision:

Categorize expenditures with precision, distinguishing between necessities and discretionary spending. This clarity facilitates targeted adjustments and ensures resources are allocated according to priorities.

3. Embrace the 50/30/20 Rule:

Consider the 50/30/20 rule as a guideline. Allocate 50% of income to essentials, 30% to discretionary spending, and 20% to savings and debt repayment. This balanced approach fosters financial stability and wealth-building simultaneously.

4. Set Achievable Goals:

Incorporate achievable financial goals into your budget. Whether it's paying off credit card debt or saving for a vacation, specific goals provide motivation and direction within your budgeting framework.

5. Regularly Review and Adjust:

Schedule regular reviews of your budget to assess its effectiveness. Life is dynamic, and financial needs evolve. Be flexible, making adjustments as necessary to align your budget with changing circumstances and goals.

6. Leverage Technology:

Explore budgeting apps and tools. These tech solutions streamline the budgeting process, providing real-time insights into your financial landscape and simplifying the tracking of income, expenses, and savings goals.

7. Prioritize Debt Repayment:

Prioritize debt repayment within your budget. Adopt strategies like the debt snowball or debt avalanche to systematically eliminate outstanding balances. Liberating yourself from debt is a transformative step toward financial freedom.

8. Emergency Fund as a Priority:

Treat your emergency fund as a budgeting priority. Establishing and consistently contributing to this fund ensures financial resilience during unexpected events, safeguarding your overall financial well-being.

9. Involve Family and Share Goals:

If applicable, involve family members in the budgeting process. Sharing financial goals fosters a sense of collective responsibility and ensures that everyone is aligned with the budget's objectives.

10. Celebrate Financial Milestones:

Celebrate achievements within your budget. Whether it's reaching a savings milestone or successfully sticking to a debt repayment plan, recognizing accomplishments reinforces positive financial habits.

By incorporating these practical tips, your budget transforms from a mere financial plan into a dynamic tool that empowers you to take charge of your financial destiny. It becomes the compass guiding you toward your goals, fostering financial security, and propelling you on the path to true financial freedom.

Tools and resources for effective budget management

Embarking on successful budget management is greatly aided by leveraging various tools and resources. Here's a comprehensive guide to the tools that can streamline your budgeting process and enhance financial control:

1. Budgeting Apps:

Mint: An all-in-one app that tracks spending, creates budgets, and provides personalized financial insights.

YNAB (You Need a Budget): Focuses on allocating every dollar purposefully, promoting a proactive approach to budgeting.

PocketGuard: Offers a straightforward overview of spending, savings, and financial goals.

2. Spreadsheets:

Microsoft Excel or Google Sheets: Customizable platforms where you can create your budget from scratch or use pre-designed templates.

3. Expense Tracking Apps:

Expensify: Ideal for tracking expenses, especially for business-related purposes.

Receipts by Wave: Simplifies receipt tracking and expense management for small business owners and freelancers.

4. Banking Apps:

Mobile Banking Apps: Many banks offer robust mobile apps that allow you to track spending, set budget limits, and receive real-time transaction alerts.

5. Investment Tracking Tools:

Personal Capital: Besides budgeting, it provides tools for tracking investments and planning for retirement.

Morningstar: Useful for in-depth analysis of your investment portfolio and performance.

6. Credit Score Monitoring:

Credit Karma: Monitors your credit score, provides credit reports, and offers personalized financial recommendations.

7. Automatic Savings Apps:

Acorns: Rounds up everyday purchases to invest the spare change automatically.

Digit: Analyzes spending patterns and transfers small amounts to a savings account.

8. Debt Repayment Tools:

Unbury.me: Helps you visualize and plan debt repayment strategies, such as the debt snowball or debt avalanche.

9. Financial Calculators:

Bankrate: Offers a range of financial calculators for mortgage, loan, credit card, and investment calculations.

10. Educational Resources:

Investopedia: Provides educational content on various financial topics, aiding in better financial decision-making.

Khan Academy Finance: Offers free, comprehensive courses on personal finance and investing.

Utilizing these tools strategically based on your specific needs can significantly enhance your ability to manage and optimize your budget effectively. Whether you prefer the simplicity of apps, the customization of spreadsheets, or a combination of both, integrating these resources empowers you to take control of your finances and work towards your financial goals.

2.2 Emergency Funds and Smart Saving

Establishing an emergency fund and adopting smart saving practices are essential pillars of financial resilience. In this section, we explore the significance of emergency funds and provide insights into cultivating a savings strategy that aligns with your financial goals.

1. Building an Emergency Fund:

An emergency fund serves as a financial safety net, providing a buffer against unexpected expenses or income disruptions. Aim to accumulate three to six months' worth of living expenses in this fund. Start by setting realistic savings goals and consistently contribute to your fund, prioritizing its growth as part of your budget.

2. Purposeful Saving:

Adopt a purposeful approach to saving by defining specific goals. Whether it's for a down payment on a home, an international vacation, or retirement, having clear objectives gives your savings a sense of direction. This clarity also enables you to allocate resources more efficiently within your budget.

3. Automated Savings:

Simplify your saving process by setting up automated transfers to your savings accounts. Many banking apps allow you to automate transfers, ensuring a consistent contribution to your emergency fund and other savings goals. Automation eliminates the need for manual transfers, promoting discipline in your saving habits.

4. Prioritizing High-Interest Debt Repayment:

Smart saving includes strategic debt management. Prioritize high-interest debt repayment to minimize interest payments and free up more resources for savings. This approach accelerates your journey towards financial security.

5. Creating Savings Buckets:

Divide your savings into specific buckets based on goals and timelines. For short-term goals, consider a separate account for easier access. Long-term goals may involve investment accounts that offer the potential for higher returns.

6. Maximizing Employer Benefits:

If applicable, take advantage of employer-sponsored benefits, such as retirement plans or matching contributions. These contributions represent a form of "free money" that accelerates your savings growth.

7. Adjusting Savings with Life Changes:

Life is dynamic, and so are your financial needs. Regularly reassess and adjust your savings contributions as your life circumstances change. This adaptability ensures that your savings strategy remains aligned with your evolving goals.

By incorporating these practices into your financial strategy, you not only fortify your financial foundation with an emergency fund but also cultivate a proactive and purposeful approach to saving. The combination of emergency funds and smart saving practices positions you to navigate unexpected challenges with confidence and work towards achieving your long-term financial aspirations.

The importance of emergency funds

In the realm of financial planning, the importance of emergency funds cannot be overstated. An emergency fund serves as a stalwart guardian, offering a shield of financial security in the face of life's unexpected twists and turns. Its significance lies in providing a robust buffer against the uncertainties that can abruptly disrupt the smooth trajectory of one's financial journey.

Picture a scenario where a sudden medical emergency arises, or employment status takes an unforeseen turn. In such critical moments, the emergency fund steps forward as a reliable safety net, standing between financial stability and potential turmoil. It is a reservoir of liquidity, ensuring swift responses to urgent needs without resorting to high-interest debt or depleting long-term investments.

Beyond mere financial implications, the importance of an emergency fund extends to emotional well-being. The peace of mind that comes from knowing there is a financial cushion for unexpected challenges cannot be understated. This peace allows for clearer decision-making, reduced stress, and the ability to confront financial decisions with confidence.

Moreover, the adaptability provided by an emergency fund is paramount. Life is dynamic, and circumstances evolve. Whether navigating career changes, family adjustments, or unforeseen expenses, an emergency fund equips individuals with the flexibility needed to weather these changes without compromising financial security.

In essence, an emergency fund is a strategic asset that transcends its monetary value. It symbolizes prudence, foresight, and the empowerment to face life's uncertainties head-on. It is not merely a financial tool; it is a testament to one's commitment to financial well-being and a foundational element in the pursuit of a secure and resilient financial future.

Strategies for building and maintaining savings

Building and maintaining savings require intentional strategies and disciplined habits. Here are effective approaches to fortify your savings and ensure their enduring growth:

1. Set Clear Savings Goals:

Begin by defining clear and achievable savings goals. Whether it's for an emergency fund, a major purchase, or retirement, having specific objectives provides direction and motivation for your savings efforts.

2. Automate Savings Contributions:

Leverage automation to make saving a seamless part of your financial routine. Set up automatic transfers to your savings account, ensuring a consistent and disciplined approach to building your financial reserves.

3. Prioritize High-Interest Debt Repayment:

Channel a portion of your resources towards repaying high-interest debts. As these debts decrease, redirect the funds towards your savings. This dual strategy eliminates financial liabilities while concurrently boosting your savings capacity.

4. Create a Realistic Budget:

Develop a comprehensive budget that aligns with your financial goals. Allocate a specific portion of your income to savings each month. A realistic budget serves as a roadmap for managing expenses and nurturing your savings habit.

5. Embrace Frugality:

Embrace a frugal lifestyle by conscientiously managing your spending. Differentiate between needs and wants, and actively seek ways to cut unnecessary expenses. Redirect the funds saved towards your savings goals.

6. Establish an Emergency Fund:

Prioritize the creation of an emergency fund to cover unforeseen expenses. This fund acts as a financial safety net, safeguarding your savings from unexpected drains and providing peace of mind.

7. Leverage Employer Benefits:

Maximize employer-sponsored benefits, especially those related to retirement savings. Contribute to employer-sponsored retirement plans, taking advantage of any matching contributions. This not only grows your retirement savings but also enhances your overall financial stability.

8. Explore High-Yield Savings Accounts:

Consider using high-yield savings accounts to maximize the interest earned on your savings. These accounts often offer better returns than traditional savings accounts, aiding in the growth of your financial reserves.

9. Periodically Review and Adjust:

Regularly assess your savings strategy and make adjustments as needed. Life circumstances, goals, and financial priorities evolve. Adapting your savings plan ensures it remains aligned with your current needs and aspirations.

10. Continuously Educate Yourself:

Stay informed about personal finance and investment strategies. Continuous education empowers you to make informed decisions about where and how to allocate your savings for optimal growth.

11. Celebrate Milestones:

Acknowledge and celebrate savings milestones along the way. Recognizing your achievements, whether it's reaching a specific savings target or successfully paying off a debt, reinforces positive financial habits.

By implementing these strategies consistently, you cultivate a resilient savings habit that not only builds financial security but also fosters a proactive and intentional approach to managing your financial resources.

Chapter 3:

Debt Elimination Strategies

In the pivotal exploration of "Money Mastery," Chapter 3 delves into pragmatic debt elimination strategies, offering a roadmap to liberate oneself from financial burdens. The chapter commences with a comprehensive understanding of various types of debt, distinguishing between high-interest and low-interest obligations.

The spotlight then shifts to the strategic deployment of the debt snowball and debt avalanche methods. The debt snowball advocates tackling smaller debts first for psychological wins, building momentum towards larger obligations. On the other hand, the debt avalanche prioritizes high-interest debts, minimizing overall interest payments.

Readers are guided through the process of assessing their debt landscape, identifying the most suitable strategy based on their financial situation and goals. Practical tips on negotiating with creditors, refinancing, and consolidating debts are outlined, providing actionable steps to expedite the debt elimination process.

The chapter concludes with a focus on cultivating positive financial habits to prevent future debt accumulation. By mastering these debt elimination strategies, readers will be empowered to navigate their financial landscape with newfound freedom and embark on a trajectory toward lasting financial well-being.

3.1 Tackling Debt Head-On

Confronting and overcoming debt requires a proactive and strategic approach. In this section, we explore effective strategies for tackling debt head-on, providing a roadmap to financial liberation.

1. Comprehensive Debt Assessment:

Begin by conducting a thorough assessment of your debts. Distinguish between high-interest and low-interest obligations, creating a clear picture of your overall debt landscape.

2. Choose Your Strategy:

Two prominent debt elimination strategies, the debt snowball and debt avalanche, offer distinct paths to debt freedom. The debt snowball involves prioritizing smaller debts for quick wins, fostering momentum. Conversely, the debt avalanche focuses on high-interest debts, minimizing overall interest payments.

3. Tailor to Your Situation:

Assess your financial situation and goals to determine the most suitable strategy. Whether aiming for psychological victories with the debt snowball or prioritizing financial efficiency with the debt avalanche, tailor your approach to align with your unique circumstances.

4. Negotiate and Consolidate:

Explore options for negotiating with creditors to potentially lower interest rates or negotiate more favorable repayment terms. Additionally, consider debt consolidation or refinancing as tools to streamline multiple debts into a more manageable structure.

5. Develop a Repayment Plan:

Craft a realistic and actionable repayment plan. Establish a budget that allocates a significant portion of your resources toward debt repayment, ensuring consistent progress toward your financial goals.

6. Cultivate Positive Financial Habits:

Beyond immediate debt elimination, focus on cultivating positive financial habits to prevent future debt accumulation. This involves prudent budgeting, disciplined spending, and strategic savings to build a resilient financial foundation.

7. Seek Professional Guidance:

If navigating complex debts or facing challenges, consider seeking professional advice. Financial counselors or debt management services can provide expert insights and guidance tailored to your specific situation.

Tackling debt head-on is not only about financial liberation but also about reclaiming control over your financial future. By implementing these strategies, you empower yourself to break free from the shackles of debt and embark on a journey toward lasting financial well-being.

Understanding different types of debt

In the realm of personal finance, understanding the nuances of various types of debt is crucial for making informed financial decisions. Here, we explore the distinctions between different forms of debt:

1. Secured Debt:

Secured debt is backed by collateral, such as a home or a car. If the borrower fails to repay, the lender can seize the collateral. Common examples include mortgages and auto loans.

2. Unsecured Debt:

Unsecured debt lacks collateral and relies on the borrower's creditworthiness. Examples include credit cards, medical bills, and personal loans. Due to the higher risk for lenders, interest rates on unsecured debt are typically higher.

3. Revolving Debt:

Revolving debt allows borrowers to repeatedly borrow up to a certain credit limit. Credit cards are a primary example of revolving debt. Payments can vary, and interest is charged on the remaining balance.

4. Installment Debt:

Installment debt involves fixed, regular payments over a specified period. Auto loans and mortgages are common installment debts. Payments consist of both principal and interest, and the debt is repaid by the end of the term.

5. Student Loans:

Specifically designed for education expenses, student loans come in federal and private forms. Federal student loans often offer more flexible repayment options and lower interest rates.

6. Mortgages:

Mortgages are long-term loans used to finance the purchase of a home. They are secured by the property itself. The terms, interest rates, and down payments can vary.

7. Auto Loans:

Auto loans finance the purchase of a vehicle, typically with a fixed interest rate and regular installment payments. The vehicle serves as collateral for the loan.

8. Credit Card Debt:

Credit card debt is a form of unsecured revolving debt. Cardholders can make purchases up to their credit limit, with the option to pay the balance in full or make minimum payments with associated interest.

9. Personal Loans:

Unsecured and typically with a fixed interest rate, personal loans can be used for various purposes, from debt consolidation to home improvements. They have fixed repayment terms.

Understanding the characteristics of each type of debt is foundational for effective financial planning. It empowers individuals to make informed decisions about borrowing, repayment strategies, and overall financial well-being.

Developing a debt repayment plan

Crafting a debt repayment plan is a strategic and empowering process that involves a comprehensive understanding of your financial landscape. Start by conducting a thorough assessment of your outstanding debts, categorizing them by type, interest rates, and total amounts owed.

Once armed with a clear overview, prioritize debts based on a strategy that aligns with your financial goals and preferences. Two common approaches include the debt snowball and debt avalanche methods. The debt snowball emphasizes paying off smaller debts first, offering psychological victories that build momentum. Conversely, the debt avalanche targets high-interest debts to minimize overall interest payments, providing a financially efficient route.

Negotiate with creditors to explore options for lowering interest rates or adjusting repayment terms. Consider debt consolidation or refinancing to streamline multiple debts into a more manageable structure.

Craft a realistic and actionable repayment plan by establishing a budget that allocates a significant portion of your resources toward debt repayment. Consistency is key, and the plan should be sustainable over the long term.

Beyond immediate debt elimination, focus on cultivating positive financial habits to prevent future debt accumulation. This involves prudent budgeting, disciplined spending, and strategic savings to build a resilient financial foundation.

If navigating complex debts or facing challenges, seeking professional advice from financial counsellors or debt management services can provide expert insights and guidance tailored to your specific situation.

Developing a debt repayment plan is not just about settling outstanding balances; it's about reclaiming control over your financial narrative and setting the stage for a more secure and liberated financial future.

3.2 Credit Score Mastery

Mastering your credit score is a vital aspect of financial empowerment and long-term fiscal health. This comprehensive guide navigates the nuances of credit scores, offering insights and strategies to optimize this crucial financial metric.

1. Understanding the Basics:

Begin by grasping the fundamentals of credit scores. Know that credit scores typically range from 300 to 850, with higher scores indicating better creditworthiness. Understand the key factors influencing your score, including payment history, credit utilization, length of credit history, types of credit, and new credit.

2. Regularly Monitor Your Credit Report:

Actively monitor your credit report for accuracy and potential discrepancies. Obtain free annual credit reports from major credit bureaus and promptly address any errors.

3. Pay Bills on Time:

The most influential factor in your credit score is your payment history. Consistently pay your bills on time, including credit cards, loans, and other financial obligations.

4. Manage Credit Utilization:

Keep your credit card balances in check to maintain a healthy credit utilization ratio. Aim to use a lower percentage of your available credit, ideally below 30%, to positively impact your score.

5. Diversify Your Credit Mix:

Embrace a diverse mix of credit types, including credit cards, installment loans, and retail accounts. A varied credit portfolio can positively contribute to your credit score.

6. Avoid Opening Too Many New Accounts:

While new credit can be beneficial, avoid opening multiple accounts in a short period. Each new application triggers a hard inquiry, which can temporarily impact your score.

7. Prioritize Long-Term Credit Relationships:

The length of your credit history matters. Prioritize maintaining long-term relationships with your credit accounts to demonstrate stability and reliability.

8. Strategically Manage Debt:

Develop a strategic approach to managing debt. Pay off high-interest debt first and consider debt consolidation if it aligns with your financial goals.

9. Settle Outstanding Debts:

Address any outstanding debts, especially those in collections. Negotiate with creditors and explore settlement options to improve your overall financial standing.

10. Utilize Credit Responsibly:

Responsible credit utilization involves using credit for necessary expenses and managing it wisely. Avoid maxing out credit cards and use credit as a tool for financial growth.

By mastering your credit score, you not only enhance your financial standing but also open doors to favorable interest rates, better loan terms, and increased financial opportunities. Consistent and informed credit management is a key pillar in the journey towards enduring financial well-being.

Tips for improving and maintaining a healthy credit score

Building and maintaining a healthy credit score is a dynamic process that goes beyond mere numerical achievement. It involves cultivating responsible financial habits and staying proactive in managing your credit profile. Here's a comprehensive guide to help you navigate this journey.

Firstly, prioritize the timely payment of bills. This fundamental practice is the cornerstone of a healthy credit score. Missing due dates can have lasting consequences, impacting your credit history and overall financial health. Setting up automatic payments or reminders is a practical way to ensure you consistently meet payment deadlines, demonstrating your reliability to creditors.

Regularly checking your credit report is equally vital. Your credit report is a living document that reflects your financial history. By reviewing it regularly, you can identify any inaccuracies or discrepancies. Take advantage of your right to one free annual credit report from major bureaus and promptly dispute any errors you discover. This ensures that your credit report accurately portrays your financial standing.

Managing credit card balances wisely is a key factor in maintaining a healthy credit score. Aim to keep your balances low relative to your credit limit, ideally below 30%. This practice, known as maintaining a low credit utilization ratio, signals responsible credit management and positively influences your credit score.

Diversifying your credit mix is another strategy to enhance your creditworthiness. Credit scoring models consider the types of credit you have, including credit cards, installment loans, and retail accounts. A diverse mix showcases your ability to manage various financial responsibilities, contributing positively to your credit profile.

When it comes to new credit accounts, exercise caution. While the prospect of additional credit may be enticing, opening new accounts too frequently can have adverse effects on your credit score. Each new credit application triggers a hard inquiry, which can temporarily lower your score. Be strategic about opening new accounts and only do so when it aligns with your overall financial strategy.

Long-term credit relationships hold weight in the eyes of credit scoring models. The length of your credit history influences your score. Therefore, prioritize maintaining older accounts, as they contribute positively to the average age of your accounts, showcasing your creditworthiness over time.

Lastly, settling outstanding debts is crucial for both your credit score and overall financial well-being. Engage with creditors to negotiate favorable terms or settlements for debts in collections. Develop a systematic plan to repay outstanding balances, demonstrating your commitment to resolving financial obligations.

In summary, improving and maintaining a healthy credit score is a multifaceted endeavor that requires ongoing attention and diligence. By prioritizing timely payments, regularly checking your credit report, managing credit card balances wisely, diversifying your credit mix, being cautious with new credit accounts, prioritizing long-term credit relationships, and settling outstanding debts, you not only enhance your credit score but also cultivate responsible financial habits that contribute to your overall financial well-being.

Utilizing credit wisely for financial growth

Credit is a powerful financial tool that, when used wisely, can facilitate economic growth, provide financial flexibility, and contribute to overall fiscal well-being. Understanding how to leverage credit responsibly is essential for navigating the complexities of personal finance. In this comprehensive exploration, we delve into the nuanced strategies and considerations for utilizing credit wisely to foster financial growth.

At its core, credit represents a financial trust extended to individuals by lenders. It enables people to access funds for various purposes, from purchasing a home to covering unexpected expenses. However, the responsible use of credit requires a strategic approach and a keen understanding of its implications.

1. Establishing a Strong Credit Foundation:

Building a strong credit foundation begins with understanding the factors that influence your credit score. Payment history, credit utilization, length of credit history, types of credit in use, and new credit accounts all play significant roles. A positive credit history opens doors to favorable interest rates, better loan terms, and increased financial opportunities.

2. Building Credit Through Responsible Habits:

Responsible credit-building habits involve timely payment of bills and judicious use of credit. Consistently paying bills on time is a fundamental practice that demonstrates financial reliability to creditors. Additionally, managing credit card balances wisely, keeping credit utilization low, and diversifying your credit mix contribute to a positive credit profile.

3. Strategic Use of Credit for Major Purchases:

The judicious use of credit can be a catalyst for major financial milestones, such as homeownership or higher education. Mortgages and student loans are examples of credit tools that empower individuals to make significant investments in their future. Strategic planning and consideration of the long-term financial impact are crucial when taking on such substantial credit obligations.

4. Credit for Small Business Growth:

For entrepreneurs and small business owners, credit can be instrumental in fueling business growth. Business credit cards, loans, and lines of credit offer financial flexibility to cover operational expenses, invest in expansion, or navigate cash flow challenges. However, it is imperative to separate personal and business finances and use business credit responsibly to avoid unnecessary risks.

5. Responsible Use of Credit Cards:

Credit cards, when used responsibly, can be valuable financial tools. They offer convenience, rewards, and the opportunity to build credit. However, it's crucial to use credit cards judiciously, paying the balance in full each month to avoid high-interest charges. Maxing out credit cards or only making minimum payments can lead to financial strain and negatively impact credit scores.

6. Emergency Preparedness and Credit:

Credit can serve as a crucial safety net during emergencies. An established credit line or credit card can provide immediate financial relief when unexpected expenses arise. However, relying on credit for emergencies underscores the importance of having an emergency fund in place to avoid accumulating high-interest debt.

7. Debt Consolidation for Financial Efficiency:

When managed strategically, debt consolidation can be a tool for financial efficiency. Combining multiple debts into a single, manageable payment can simplify financial obligations and potentially lower interest rates. However, individuals considering debt consolidation should carefully evaluate the terms, fees, and overall impact on their financial situation.

8. Continuous Monitoring and Adjustment:

Utilizing credit wisely requires ongoing monitoring and adjustment. Regularly reviewing credit reports ensures accuracy and allows for prompt resolution of any discrepancies. Additionally, periodically reassessing financial goals and adjusting credit usage accordingly ensures alignment with broader financial strategies.

In conclusion, utilizing credit wisely for financial growth is a nuanced and strategic endeavor. It involves building a strong credit foundation, fostering responsible credit habits, strategically using credit for major purchases or business growth, and continuously monitoring and adjusting credit strategies. When approached with care and foresight, credit becomes a valuable ally in achieving financial goals and cultivating a stable and prosperous financial future.

Chapter 4:

Investing for Long-Term Wealth

In the pursuit of financial freedom, investing for long-term wealth emerges as a cornerstone strategy. This chapter navigates the intricacies of making informed investment decisions that transcend immediate gains, focusing on building enduring prosperity.

The journey begins with a fundamental exploration of investment principles. Readers delve into the concept of risk and reward, understanding that prudent investment involves a balance between potential returns and the associated risks. The chapter emphasizes the significance of aligning investments with individual financial goals, time horizons, and risk tolerance.

Diversification takes center stage as a risk management strategy. Readers discover the power of spreading investments across different asset classes to mitigate the impact of market fluctuations. The chapter guides them through the selection of diversified investment vehicles, from stocks and bonds to real estate and alternative investments.

A profound understanding of the compounding effect underscores the chapter's narrative. Readers grasp the transformative potential of allowing investments to grow over time, leveraging not only the initial capital but also the accumulated returns. The chapter introduces key investment vehicles that harness compounding, such as tax-advantaged retirement accounts and long-term investment portfolios.

The narrative extends to the significance of staying informed about market trends and adjusting investment strategies accordingly. By advocating for a proactive approach, the chapter empowers readers to adapt to changing economic landscapes and make well-informed decisions.

As the chapter unfolds, it unravels the realm of retirement planning and the critical role that investments play in securing a comfortable and financially stable retirement. From understanding retirement accounts to implementing sound investment strategies, readers are equipped with the knowledge to navigate this pivotal phase of financial planning.

Ultimately, "Investing for Long-Term Wealth" serves as a guide for readers to transcend the allure of quick wins and embrace a patient and strategic approach to wealth accumulation. By instilling the principles of diversified, compounding investments aligned with individual financial objectives, this chapter lays the foundation for a resilient and prosperous financial future.

4.1 The Power of Compound Interest

In the realm of financial growth and wealth accumulation, few concepts wield as much transformative power as compound interest. Often hailed as the "eighth wonder of the world" by Albert Einstein, compound interest has the potential to turn modest investments into substantial wealth over time. Understanding and harnessing this force is pivotal for individuals seeking to secure their financial future.

At its essence, compound interest is the interest earned not only on the initial principal but also on the accumulated interest from previous periods. This compounding effect results in a snowballing growth of wealth, with each interest payment contributing to an expanding base for future earnings. The magic lies in the exponential nature of this growth, where the longer the money is allowed to compound, the more significant the impact.

The key to unlocking the power of compound interest is time. Time allows for the multiplication of earnings, with each compounding period building upon the previous one. This underscores the importance of starting to invest early, as it maximizes the time available for compounding to work its magic. Even modest contributions can lead to substantial wealth accumulation when given enough time to compound.

Consider two scenarios: one where an individual begins investing at the age of 25 and another who starts at 35. Both invest the same amount annually, but the early starter benefits significantly more from the compounding effect. The extra ten years of compounding can result in a substantially larger investment portfolio for the individual who began earlier, showcasing the exponential impact of time on wealth growth.

To fully grasp the power of compound interest, it's essential to appreciate its role in various financial instruments. One notable example is retirement accounts, such as 401(k)s or IRAs. These accounts offer a tax-advantaged environment where investments can compound without the drag of annual taxes. Contributions to these accounts not only benefit from the compounding effect but also from potential tax deductions, providing a double advantage.

The compounding effect is equally pronounced in the world of savings and investments. Whether through stocks, bonds, or other investment vehicles, allowing returns to reinvest and compound over time amplifies the growth potential. This compounding phenomenon not only applies to interest but also to dividends and capital gains, further enhancing the overall wealth accumulation.

While compound interest is a powerful ally in wealth-building, it's crucial to acknowledge its counterpart—compound debt. The same compounding principle applies to debts, where interest accrues not just on the principal but on the accumulated interest as well. This is why addressing high-interest debts promptly is essential, as it prevents the compounding effect from working against financial well-being.

The concept of compound interest extends beyond traditional investment accounts. It permeates various aspects of personal finance, including savings accounts, education funds, and real estate investments. In each scenario, the disciplined application of the compounding principle serves as a force multiplier, elevating the potential for financial growth.

In conclusion, the power of compound interest is a financial phenomenon that can shape the trajectory of wealth accumulation. Time, discipline, and strategic financial planning are the keys to unlocking its full potential. By starting early, making consistent contributions, and allowing investments to compound over the long term, individuals can harness the exponential growth offered by compound interest and pave the way for a financially secure and prosperous future.

Explaining the impact of compounding on investments

In the intricate landscape of finance, the concept of compounding stands as a potent force, capable of reshaping the dynamics of wealth accumulation. When applied to investments, compounding becomes a silent but powerful ally, working tirelessly to multiply wealth over time. Understanding the profound impact of compounding on investments is essential for individuals navigating the path to financial prosperity.

At its core, compounding involves the process of earning interest not just on the initial principal amount but also on the accumulated interest from previous periods. This compounding effect sets in motion a virtuous cycle, where each interest payment contributes to an expanding base for future earnings. The beauty of compounding lies in its ability to generate exponential growth, turning the seemingly modest contributions into substantial wealth.

The cornerstone of compounding's impact is time. Time is the catalyst that allows the multiplication of earnings, with each compounding period building upon the previous one. This underscores a fundamental truth in the world of investing: the earlier one starts, the more significant the impact of compounding.

Consider two hypothetical scenarios to illustrate this point. In the first scenario, an individual begins investing $1,000 annually at the age of 25, while in the second scenario, another individual starts investing the same amount at the age of 35. Both individuals invest for 40 years. Despite investing the same annual amount, the person who began at 25 benefits significantly more from the compounding effect. The extra ten years of compounding results in a substantially larger investment portfolio, showcasing the exponential impact of time on wealth growth.

To appreciate the impact of compounding, it's crucial to understand its role in various financial instruments. Retirement accounts, such as 401(k)s or IRAs, exemplify the power of compounding. These accounts offer a tax-advantaged environment where investments can compound without the annual drag of taxes. Contributions not only benefit from the compounding effect but also from potential tax deductions, providing a double advantage.

In the realm of savings and investments, compounding amplifies the growth potential. Whether through stocks, bonds, or other investment vehicles, allowing returns to reinvest and compound over time enhances the overall wealth accumulation. This compounding phenomenon applies not only to interest but also to dividends and capital gains, further bolstering the transformative impact on the investment portfolio.

To illustrate, consider an investment with an average annual return of 8%. In the first year, the compounding effect generates earnings on the initial investment. In the second year, it generates earnings not just on the initial investment but also on the earnings from the first year. As this process repeats over the years, the compounding effect accelerates, leading to a more pronounced growth curve.

While compounding serves as a powerful ally in wealth-building, it's imperative to recognize its counterpart—compound debt. Just as investments benefit from compounding, debts incur compound interest, where interest accumulates not just on the principal but also on the accumulated interest. Addressing high-interest debts promptly is crucial to prevent the compounding effect from working against financial well-being.

The application of the compounding principle extends beyond traditional investment accounts. It permeates various aspects of personal finance, including savings accounts, education funds, and real estate investments. In each scenario, disciplined and strategic application of the compounding principle serves as a force multiplier, elevating the potential for financial growth.

The concept of compounding is not solely about numerical growth; it also aligns with the psychological aspect of investing. As individuals witness the compounding effect over time, it instills a sense of confidence and discipline in their investment approach. This reinforcement of positive financial habits becomes a driving force in the journey toward financial prosperity.

In conclusion, explaining the impact of compounding on investments unveils a financial phenomenon that transcends mere numerical calculations. It is a dynamic force that, when harnessed strategically and coupled with time, has the potential to reshape the financial landscape. By grasping the exponential nature of compounding and incorporating it into investment strategies, individuals can unlock a powerful mechanism for building enduring wealth and securing a prosperous financial future.

Choosing the right investment vehicles

In the multifaceted world of investments, selecting the right vehicles is a pivotal step on the path to financial growth and security. The array of available options, from stocks and bonds to real estate and mutual funds, can be both empowering and overwhelming. Understanding the nuances of each investment vehicle and aligning them with individual financial goals is essential for constructing a robust and diversified investment portfolio.

One of the foundational choices in investing is between stocks and bonds, each offering distinct characteristics and risk-reward profiles. Stocks represent ownership in a company, entitling the investor to a share of its profits. While stocks can offer substantial returns, they are also associated with higher volatility and risk. On the other hand, bonds are debt instruments where investors lend money to an entity, such as a government or corporation, in exchange for periodic interest payments and the return of the principal at maturity. Bonds are generally considered more stable than stocks but may offer lower returns.

Mutual funds and exchange-traded funds (ETFs) present an alternative approach, allowing investors to pool their money into a diversified portfolio managed by professionals. Mutual funds are actively managed, meaning fund managers make decisions about asset allocation and security selection. ETFs, on the other hand, typically passively track a specific index, providing a cost-effective and transparent investment option. Both vehicles offer diversification, reducing the risk associated with individual securities.

Real estate stands as a tangible and potentially lucrative investment. It encompasses a spectrum of options, including residential and commercial properties, real estate investment trusts (REITs), and rental properties. Real estate investments can provide a source of regular income through rent and the potential for property appreciation over time. However, real estate investments require careful consideration of market conditions, property management, and economic factors.

Retirement accounts, such as 401(k)s and Individual Retirement Accounts (IRAs), are crucial investment vehicles designed to support long-term financial goals. These accounts offer tax advantages, allowing contributions to grow tax-deferred or tax-free. Traditional 401(k)s and IRAs provide tax deductions on contributions, while Roth versions allow for tax-free withdrawals in retirement. Leveraging retirement accounts ensures a disciplined approach to long-term investing and capitalizes on compounding growth.

For those seeking a hands-on approach, individual stocks provide a direct stake in specific companies. This approach requires thorough research and a deep understanding of the chosen companies and industries. Investing in individual stocks can offer the potential for significant returns, but it comes with higher risk and demands active portfolio management.

Diversification, a cornerstone of sound investment strategy, involves spreading investments across various asset classes to mitigate risk. This principle aligns with the proverb, "Don't put all your eggs in one basket." Diversified portfolios encompass a mix of stocks, bonds, real estate, and other assets to balance risk and potential returns. Diversification is achieved not only through the selection of different investment vehicles but also by investing across various industries, geographic regions, and sectors.

Understanding risk tolerance is paramount in choosing the right investment vehicles. Risk tolerance is an individual's ability to withstand fluctuations in the value of their investments.

Factors such as age, financial goals, and comfort with volatility influence risk tolerance. Younger investors with a longer time horizon may lean towards more aggressive, growth-oriented investments, while those closer to retirement may prioritize capital preservation and income generation.

The emergence of robo-advisors adds a technological dimension to investment decisions. These automated platforms use algorithms to create and manage diversified portfolios based on individual risk profiles and financial goals. Robo-advisors provide a low-cost and accessible entry point for investors, particularly those who prefer a hands-off approach to portfolio management.

Staying informed about market trends and economic indicators is essential for making informed investment decisions. Regular monitoring allows investors to adapt their strategies in response to changing market conditions. Economic factors, interest rates, and geopolitical events can impact the performance of various investment vehicles, necessitating a proactive and informed approach.

In conclusion, choosing the right investment vehicles is a dynamic and personalized process. It involves a careful consideration of financial goals, risk tolerance, and time horizon. Constructing a diversified portfolio that aligns with these factors can help investors navigate market fluctuations and work towards their long-term financial objectives. Whether opting for stocks, bonds, mutual funds, real estate, or a combination of these, the key is to approach investment decisions with a strategic mindset and a commitment to ongoing financial education.

4.2 Diversification and Risk Management

In the complex landscape of investing, the principles of diversification and risk management emerge as essential strategies for building a resilient and balanced investment portfolio. Diversification involves spreading investments across a range of asset classes, industries, and geographic regions to mitigate the impact of any single investment's poor performance. This approach aims to strike a balance between potential returns and the associated risks.

The primary goal of diversification is to reduce the overall volatility of a portfolio. By holding a mix of assets that may respond differently to various economic conditions, the impact of a downturn in one sector can be offset by the positive performance of others. For example, during periods of economic growth, stocks may outperform bonds, while in economic downturns, bonds may provide a more stable source of returns.

Diversification is not only about the selection of different types of investments but also about spreading risk within each asset class. Within the stock portion of a portfolio, investors may diversify by investing in different industries or market sectors. Similarly, within the bond portion, diversification can be achieved by holding bonds with different maturities and credit qualities.

Risk management is inherently tied to diversification, and both concepts work in tandem to protect and enhance an investment portfolio. Understanding and assessing risk tolerance is a fundamental step in constructing a diversified portfolio that aligns with an investor's financial goals and comfort with market fluctuations.

While diversification can help mitigate risks, it's important to note that it does not eliminate them entirely. External factors such as economic recessions, market shocks, and global events can impact various asset classes simultaneously. Therefore, staying informed about market trends, economic indicators, and global events is crucial for making informed decisions and adjusting investment strategies as needed.

Investors should periodically review and rebalance their portfolios to ensure that the original diversification strategy remains intact. Market fluctuations may cause the allocation of assets to shift, deviating from the intended balance. Rebalancing involves selling assets that have outperformed and using the proceeds to purchase assets that may be underrepresented. This disciplined approach helps investors maintain their desired risk-return profile.

Diversification and risk management are particularly relevant in times of market uncertainty. They provide a framework for investors to navigate volatile periods with a measured and strategic approach. By embracing the principles of diversification, investors can enhance the potential for long-term growth while managing the inherent risks associated with the dynamic nature of financial markets.

In essence, the combination of diversification and risk management represents a prudent and calculated approach to investing. It acknowledges that markets are inherently unpredictable, and by spreading investments strategically and actively managing risks, investors can build a more resilient portfolio capable of weathering various market conditions.

Strategies for building a diversified investment portfolio

Constructing a diversified investment portfolio is a strategic endeavor that involves careful consideration of various factors to achieve a balance between potential returns and risk mitigation. Diversification is a cornerstone principle that recognizes the unpredictability of financial markets and seeks to spread investments across different asset classes, industries, and geographic regions.

One key strategy for building a diversified portfolio is asset allocation. This involves determining the proportion of assets allocated to different categories, such as stocks, bonds, and cash equivalents. The appropriate allocation depends on individual financial goals, risk tolerance, and time horizon. Younger investors with a longer time horizon may lean towards a more aggressive allocation with a higher percentage in stocks, while those closer to retirement may prioritize a more conservative mix that includes a higher allocation to bonds.

Within each asset class, further diversification can be achieved by selecting a range of investments. For example, in the stock portion of the portfolio, investors can diversify by choosing stocks from different industries and market sectors. Similarly, within the bond portion, diversification can be accomplished by holding bonds with different maturities and credit qualities.

Investors may also consider diversifying across geographic regions to mitigate risks associated with economic and geopolitical factors in any single country. International diversification provides exposure to a broader range of opportunities and can enhance the overall stability of the portfolio.

The use of investment vehicles such as mutual funds and exchange-traded funds (ETFs) is another effective strategy for diversification. These funds pool money from multiple investors to invest in a diversified portfolio of stocks, bonds, or other assets. They offer an efficient way to access a broad range of investments without the need for individual security selection.

Risk management is integral to the diversification process. Understanding and assessing risk tolerance helps investors construct a portfolio that aligns with their comfort level for market fluctuations. A well-diversified portfolio should be designed to weather various economic conditions and market cycles, helping to protect against the impact of poor performance in any single investment.

Regular portfolio reviews and rebalancing are essential to maintaining the intended diversification strategy. Market fluctuations may cause the allocation of assets to deviate from the original plan. Rebalancing involves selling assets that have outperformed and reallocating the proceeds to assets that may be underrepresented. This disciplined approach ensures that the portfolio remains aligned with the investor's risk-return objectives.

Staying informed about market trends, economic indicators, and global events is crucial for making informed decisions and adjusting the investment strategy as needed. Diversification is not a one-time task but an ongoing process that requires attention and adaptation to changing market conditions.

In conclusion, building a diversified investment portfolio involves a thoughtful and dynamic approach. By strategically allocating assets, diversifying within each asset class, considering international exposure, utilizing investment vehicles, and actively managing risk through regular reviews and rebalancing, investors can construct a resilient portfolio capable of navigating the complexities of the financial markets. The goal is to create a well-balanced and adaptable investment strategy that aligns with individual financial objectives and withstands the unpredictable nature of the investment landscape.

Mitigating risks in investment decisions

There will always be a measure of risk in investing, and successful investors understand that protecting their portfolios requires minimizing those risks. Risk cannot be eliminated entirely, but through such strategic measures negative impacts can be minimized on investment returns.

A basic risk reduction strategy is diversification. It means making investments in different types of assets, industries and geographic areas. The idea is not to put all eggs in one basket, spreading the impact of bad performance out across a number of separate investments. This is a basic principle of risk management; it helps create a more balanced and safer portfolio.

Asset allocation is intimately related to diversification and involves deciding upon the proportion of different asset classes held in a portfolio. Asset allocation based on individual financial objectives, risk tolerance and time horizon allows investors to create a balanced portfolio suited precisely for their own needs. So, for example, a conservative investor may choose to increase investment in bonds (which are generally regarded as less volatile than stocks).

Proper research and due diligence are important aspects of effective risk-mitigation. Before making any investment decisions, investors must thoroughly study potential opportunities. This means scrutinizing the financial health of firms, paying attention to market trends and monitoring economic indicators. Informed decision-making is a potent weapon against the uncertainties accompanying investment decisions.

Setting reasonable expectations is part and parcel of risk management. Therefore, investors need to be aware of the expected returns and risks from their chosen investments. If expectations are unreasonable, people make poor decisions and become more vulnerable to market fluctuations. Such a realistic outlook helps investors keep their eyes trained on the goal and avoid getting caught up in short-term market variations.

Regular monitoring and assessment of the investment portfolio are crucial for effective risk management. Markets are dynamic, and economic conditions can change rapidly. Periodic reviews allow investors to identify and address potential risks in a timely manner. This includes reassessing the portfolio's asset allocation, rebalancing when necessary, and staying attuned to any shifts in market conditions.

Utilizing risk management tools, such as stop-loss orders, can help protect investments from significant downturns. A stop-loss order sets a predetermined price at which a security will be sold to limit losses. While it may result in selling an investment at a loss, it provides a mechanism for preventing more substantial declines in value.

Risk management also involves recognizing the importance of liquidity. Having a portion of the portfolio in liquid assets ensures the ability to meet financial needs or take advantage of investment opportunities, especially in challenging market conditions. Liquidity provides flexibility and reduces the risk of forced selling at unfavorable prices.

Lastly, cultivating a disciplined and patient approach is integral to effective risk management. Emotions can play a significant role in investment decisions, and impulsive reactions to market fluctuations can lead to suboptimal outcomes. A disciplined investor adheres to a well-thought-out investment strategy, avoiding knee-jerk reactions and staying focused on long-term goals.

In conclusion, mitigating risks in investment decisions is a multifaceted process that requires a combination of strategies. Diversification, asset allocation, thorough research, realistic expectations, regular monitoring, risk management tools, attention to liquidity, and disciplined decision-making collectively contribute to a robust risk management framework. Successful investors understand that while risks cannot be eliminated entirely, they can be prudently managed to create a resilient and adaptive investment strategy.

Chapter 5:

Passive Income Streams

Passive income is a financial concept that holds great appeal for individuals seeking to diversify their income sources and achieve greater financial independence. Unlike active income, which requires ongoing effort and time to generate, passive income streams are designed to generate revenue with minimal ongoing effort or direct involvement. Building passive income streams is a strategic approach to financial stability and creating avenues for wealth accumulation.

One of the most common forms of passive income is through investments, such as dividends from stocks or interest from bonds. When investors allocate funds to income-generating assets, they earn a share of the profits without actively managing the day-to-day operations of the underlying businesses. This allows individuals to benefit from the performance of their investments while having the flexibility to pursue other endeavors.

Real estate investments represent another robust avenue for passive income. Rental properties, real estate crowdfunding, and real estate investment trusts (REITs) offer opportunities for individuals to earn regular income through property ownership without being directly involved in property management. The potential for property appreciation further enhances the long-term financial benefits of real estate investments.

Building and monetizing a blog or website is a contemporary method of generating passive income. Through affiliate marketing, sponsored content, or digital product sales, content creators can establish revenue streams that continue to generate income even when they are not actively creating new content. Over time, a well-established online presence can become a sustainable source of passive income.

Creating and selling digital products, such as e-books, online courses, or stock photography, is another avenue for generating passive income. Once the initial product is developed and marketed, individuals can continue to earn income from sales without the need for ongoing production or direct customer interaction. This scalable approach allows creators to reach a global audience and capitalize on their expertise.

Dividend-paying stocks and mutual funds offer an attractive passive income option for investors. Companies that distribute a portion of their profits to shareholders in the form of dividends provide investors with a regular income stream. By strategically selecting dividend-paying investments, individuals can establish a reliable source of passive income that complements their overall financial strategy.

Licensing intellectual property, such as patents, trademarks, or copyrighted works, provides an opportunity for creators to earn passive income through royalties. Licensing agreements allow individuals to grant others the right to use their intellectual property in exchange for ongoing payments. This passive income stream is particularly prevalent in industries such as technology, entertainment, and publishing.

Establishing a business with effective systems and delegation in place can transform active income into passive income. Once the business is operational and can function without constant hands-on involvement, entrepreneurs can step back from day-to-day operations while still reaping the financial rewards. This approach requires initial effort to build a solid foundation but offers the potential for long-term passive income.

In conclusion, passive income streams are a powerful mechanism for achieving financial freedom and building wealth over time. Whether through investments, real estate, online ventures, digital products, or business ownership, individuals can strategically diversify their income sources and create sustainable avenues for generating revenue. Passive income not only provides financial stability but also offers the freedom to pursue other interests and priorities, ultimately contributing to a more balanced and fulfilling lifestyle.

5.1 Creating Passive Income Opportunities

In the quest for financial independence and a more flexible lifestyle, the creation of passive income opportunities stands as a strategic and empowering approach. Passive income, earned with minimal effort or direct involvement, opens avenues for individuals to diversify their income streams and build wealth over time. Crafting and nurturing passive income opportunities requires a combination of creativity, strategic planning, and a willingness to invest time and resources upfront for long-term gains.

Investing in income-generating assets, such as stocks or bonds, serves as a traditional yet effective method to create passive income. Dividends from stocks and interest from bonds provide a steady stream of income for investors, allowing them to benefit from the performance of well-chosen assets without the need for active management. This approach requires thoughtful portfolio construction and an understanding of the risk-return profile of different investments.

Real estate investments offer a tangible and potentially lucrative avenue for passive income. Owning rental properties, participating in real estate crowdfunding, or investing in real estate investment trusts (REITs) allows individuals to generate regular income from property ownership without hands-on property management. The appreciation of real estate assets further enhances the long-term financial benefits.

Building an online presence through blogging or creating a niche website provides opportunities for passive income through various channels. Affiliate marketing, sponsored content, and digital product sales allow content creators to monetize their online platforms. Over time, as the audience grows and content accumulates, these digital assets can become reliable sources of passive income.

Developing and selling digital products, such as e-books, online courses, or software, is a scalable method to create passive income. Once the initial product is created and marketed, individuals can continue to earn income from sales without the need for ongoing production or direct customer interaction. This approach leverages expertise and creativity to establish revenue streams that persist over time.

Investing in dividend-paying stocks and mutual funds provides a reliable source of passive income. Companies that distribute a portion of their profits to shareholders through dividends offer investors a regular income stream. By strategically selecting dividend-paying investments, individuals can build a diversified portfolio that generates consistent passive income while benefiting from the potential for capital appreciation.

Licensing intellectual property is a pathway to passive income for creators. By licensing patents, trademarks, or copyrighted works, individuals grant others the right to use their intellectual property in exchange for ongoing payments or royalties. This approach allows creators to monetize their intellectual assets without the need for continuous direct involvement.

Creating a business with effective systems and delegation in place can transform active income into passive income. As the business matures and can operate with minimal day-to-day involvement, entrepreneurs can step back while the business continues to generate revenue. This approach necessitates initial effort to establish efficient operations but offers the potential for sustainable passive income.

In summary, creating passive income opportunities requires a proactive and strategic approach. Whether through investments, real estate, online ventures, digital products, or business ownership, individuals can diversify their income sources and lay the foundation for long-term financial success. While the initial investment of time and resources is significant, the potential for ongoing passive income provides financial stability, freedom, and the opportunity to pursue a more balanced and fulfilling life.

Exploring various passive income streams

Passive income, often considered the holy grail of financial freedom, offers individuals the opportunity to diversify their income streams and build wealth with minimal ongoing effort. Here, we delve into various passive income streams, each presenting unique avenues for financial growth:

1. Investing in Income-Generating Assets:

- Dividends from stocks and interest from bonds provide a steady stream of income for investors without requiring active management.
- Constructing a well-balanced investment portfolio is essential for optimizing passive income potential.

2. Real Estate Investments:

- Owning rental properties, participating in real estate crowdfunding, or investing in Real Estate Investment Trusts (REITs) can generate regular passive income.

- Real estate assets offer the potential for both income and long-term appreciation.

3. Online Ventures:

- Creating and monetizing a blog, website, or YouTube channel allows individuals to earn through affiliate marketing, sponsored content, and digital product sales.
- The growth of an online presence transforms these platforms into sustainable sources of passive income.

4. Digital Products:

- Developing and selling digital products like e-books, online courses, or stock photography provides scalable passive income opportunities.
- Once created, digital products can be sold repeatedly without the need for continuous production.

5. Dividend-Paying Stocks and Mutual Funds:

- Investing in companies that distribute profits to shareholders through dividends offers a consistent and predictable income stream.
- Strategically selecting such investments contributes to building a diversified portfolio for passive income.

6. Licensing Intellectual Property:

- Creators can earn passive income by licensing patents, trademarks, or copyrighted works, allowing others to use intellectual property in exchange for ongoing payments.
- This approach enables creators to monetize their innovations without constant involvement.

7. Business Ownership with Effective Systems:

- Establishing a business with streamlined systems and effective delegation allows entrepreneurs to transform active income into passive income.
- As the business matures and operates independently, it continues to generate revenue with reduced direct involvement.

Exploring these various passive income streams requires a tailored approach based on individual preferences, risk tolerance, and financial goals. Diversifying across multiple streams can provide resilience and create a robust financial portfolio, ultimately offering the freedom to live life on one's own terms.

Building a plan for passive income generation

Creating a comprehensive plan for passive income generation is a strategic endeavor that involves careful consideration of financial goals, risk tolerance, and a diversified approach. Here's a step-by-step guide to building a robust plan for cultivating passive income streams:

1. Set Clear Financial Goals:

- Define specific and measurable financial objectives. Whether it's achieving a certain level of monthly passive income or funding a particular lifestyle, clarity in goals is the foundation of the plan.

2. Assess Current Financial Situation:

- Evaluate existing income, expenses, and assets. Understanding the current financial landscape provides insights into how passive income can complement and enhance overall financial stability.

3. Identify Preferred Passive Income Streams:

- Explore various passive income streams such as investments, real estate, online ventures, or intellectual property. Select streams that align with personal interests, expertise, and long-term objectives.

4. Diversify Income Sources:

- Avoid reliance on a single income stream. Diversification minimizes risk and enhances the resilience of the passive income plan. Consider a mix of investments, business ownership, and digital ventures.

5. Research and Education:

- Invest time in researching chosen income streams. Stay informed about market trends, risks, and potential returns. Continuous learning is crucial for making informed decisions in the dynamic landscape of passive income generation.

6. Create a Realistic Timeline:

- Establish a realistic timeline for achieving passive income goals. Understand that building sustainable streams takes time. A phased approach with short-term and long-term milestones can provide a sense of progress.

7. Allocate Resources:

- Allocate financial resources for initial investments, business setup, or product development. Balancing the allocation based on risk tolerance and expected returns is integral to a well-rounded plan.

8. Implement Risk Management Strategies:

- Identify potential risks associated with chosen income streams and develop mitigation strategies. This may involve diversification, setting stop-loss orders, or having contingency plans in place.

9. Monitor and Adjust:

- Regularly monitor the performance of passive income streams. Assess the effectiveness of the plan and be prepared to adjust strategies based on changing market conditions or personal circumstances.

10. Reinvest Profits for Growth:

- Consider reinvesting a portion of passive income profits to fuel further growth. Reinvestment can enhance the scalability and longevity of income streams over time.

11. Review and Revise the Plan Periodically:

- Life circumstances, market conditions, and financial goals can change. Periodically review and revise the passive income plan to ensure it remains aligned with evolving objectives.

12. Seek Professional Advice:

- Consult with financial advisors, tax professionals, or experts in chosen fields to gain insights and optimize strategies. Professional advice can provide valuable guidance for a well-informed passive income plan.

Building a plan for passive income generation requires a thoughtful and disciplined approach. By setting clear goals, diversifying income sources, staying informed, and adapting strategies over time, individuals can cultivate a reliable and sustainable flow of passive income, ultimately paving the way toward financial freedom and flexibility.

5.2 Real Estate and Other Investment Opportunities

Properly investing is one of the pillars upon which financial success stands, and real estate continues to be a strong foundation over long periods for building wealth. Aside from traditional investment choices, real estate offers a concrete and flexible way to build equity; generate rental income; benefit from rising property prices.

Real Estate Investment:

Real estate investment means buying, owning and exploiting property in order to obtain a return. From residential properties to commercial spaces and even vacation rentals, these represent all kinds of options in real estate. Apart from the possibility of capital appreciation through time, real estate also offers a stable source of cash flow that can be provided by renting out properties.

Rental Income:

Rental income is one of the biggest advantages real estate investment has to offer. When investors lease properties out to tenants, they can create a predictable cash flow that helps pay the mortgage and other operating costs. Rental income is not only immediate return in cash. It also accrues equity over the long term.

Property Appreciation:

Property values have always risen as time goes by, so owning property is a mode of building wealth. Real estate, however turbulent the market at any given time can be a powerful medium for investment. Well-placed real estate investments based on strategic consideration and thorough research often generate significant returns in property value appreciation alone.

Diversification with Real Estate Investment Trusts (REITs):

However, for persons trying to get the advantages of real property with out all its baggage, Real Estate Investment Trusts (REIT) provide an incredible substitute. REITs are funding cars which gather the price range of many buyers and make investments them in a diversified portfolio of actual property belongings. Investors can enjoy not most effective apartment income but additionally probable expanded property values with much less control problem.

Alternative Investments:

Alternative Investments Aside from conventional actual property, there are different funding possibilities for diversification. That will be an investment in a startup, personal fairness or hedge fund. Because alternative investments typically have a one-of-a-kind danger-go back feature than conventional assets, they provide any other way to similarly stabilize and diversify an investment portfolio.

Stock Market Investments:

Investing in publicly traded agencies is a traditional manner to build up wealth. From blue-chip shares to boom offerings, the inventory marketplace provides many alternatives for buyers. By being able to take benefit of a prospect for capital appreciation and dividends, investors can boom their wealth through the years.

Cryptocurrency and Digital Assets:

The start of virtual assets such as Bitcoin and Ethereum has unfolded a new frontier for funding. Digital belongings are not as valid or relied on, but they do provide a decentralized and without borders funding for those searching for to diversify their portfolios.

Balancing Risk and Reward:

Successful investment techniques often hinge on finding the right stability between chance and praise. Diversifying throughout actual property, traditional investments, and alternative belongings can mitigate dangers associated with marketplace volatility and financial uncertainties. Each funding opportunity have to align with an investor's threat tolerance, financial goals, and ordinary wealth-building method.

In conclusion, actual property and other funding possibilities offer avenues for people to grow their wealth and secure their financial futures. Whether via the regular profits of rental houses, the capacity for assets appreciation, or diversification into alternative property, thoughtful funding selections can yield each immediately and long-term monetary advantages. As with any funding, cautious studies, due diligence, and a strategic technique are essential to maximizing returns and mitigating risks.

The role of real estate in wealth creation

Real property, with its precise traits and long-time period capacity, performs a pivotal position in wealth introduction for individuals and buyers. Beyond presenting shelter, actual property offers a multifaceted technique to building and gathering wealth via various mechanisms:

1. Equity Building Through Property Ownership:

Property ownership permits individuals to build equity over the years. As loan payments are made, the quantity of fairness—the distinction between the assets's marketplace cost and the top notch mortgage—regularly increases. This equity serves as a form of compelled financial savings and contributes to normal net well worth.

2. Rental Income as a Steady Cash Flow:

Real property provides the opportunity to generate rental income by using leasing out homes to tenants. This apartment profits can function a reliable and regular coins glide, contributing to masking loan payments, assets protection charges, and probably yielding a profit.

3. Leverage and Mortgage Financing:

Real property uniquely allows for the usage of leverage through mortgage financing. By making an investment a portion of the property's overall fee as a down charge, investors can manage a larger asset. As belongings values admire, the go back on funding isn't always best primarily based on the preliminary investment but on the whole property price.

4. Property Appreciation Over Time:

Real property values have traditionally liked over the long time. While market conditions can range, strategic real property investments in regions with increase potential or improved call for can bring about tremendous appreciation. This capital appreciation complements normal wealth and gives opportunities for profitable assets sales.

5. Tax Advantages for Real Estate Investors:

Real estate investments often come with tax advantages that make a contribution to wealth introduction. Deductions for loan hobby, property taxes, and depreciation can mitigate taxable condo earnings. Additionally, profits from the sale of a number one house may be eligible for capital profits tax exclusions.

6. Diversification of Investment Portfolio:

Including real property in an investment portfolio provides diversification, spreading chance throughout different asset instructions. Real estate's overall performance is not continually without delay correlated with the inventory marketplace, presenting a buffer in opposition to marketplace volatility and financial fluctuations.

7. Real Estate Investment Trusts (REITs):

For the ones seeking publicity to actual property without direct property ownership, Real Estate Investment Trusts (REITs) provide a liquid and on hand funding alternative. REITs pool funds from multiple investors to put money into a diverse portfolio of income-generating actual estate assets, providing an road for passive income and capacity capital gains.

8. Inheritance and Legacy Building:

Real property serves as a tangible asset that can be exceeded down thru generations, contributing to the introduction of a lasting legacy. Inherited properties may be held for persevered wealth accumulation or offered to provide monetary aid to heirs.

In precis, real estate's role in wealth creation is multifaceted, encompassing equity constructing, rental earnings, leverage, assets appreciation, tax blessings, portfolio diversification, and legacy constructing. While the real estate marketplace may have its demanding situations, strategic and knowledgeable investment decisions can position individuals to harness the total wealth-constructing potential that actual property gives over the long time.

Identifying alternative investment options

In a dynamic economic panorama, buyers are increasingly exploring alternative investment alternatives to diversify their portfolios and searching for new avenues for capacity returns. Alternative investments move beyond traditional stocks and bonds, imparting unique possibilities which could complement and decorate a properly-rounded funding strategy. Here are a few key opportunity funding alternatives to recall:

1. Private Equity:

Private fairness includes making an investment in privately held corporations that are not publicly traded. This investment can take the form of direct investments, venture capital, or participation in personal fairness price range. Private equity investments often purpose to support corporations throughout their early degrees or facilitate their boom and expansion.

2. Venture Capital:

Venture capital specializes in making an investment in early-stage groups with excessive growth ability. Venture capitalists provide funding to startups in alternate for fairness, with the expectancy of vast returns if the business enterprise succeeds. While excessive-chance, a hit ventures can yield significant profits.

3. Hedge Funds:

Hedge budget are funding price range that employ numerous strategies to generate returns for his or her buyers. These techniques can include lengthy and short positions, leverage, and derivatives trading. Hedge funds are usually open to accredited investors and intention to provide absolute returns no matter market conditions.

4. Real Assets:

Investing in real assets, including commodities, valuable metals, or agricultural land, gives a tangible and frequently inflation-resistant funding alternative. Real assets can act as a hedge towards financial uncertainties and provide diversification past conventional financial contraptions.

5. Cryptocurrencies and Digital Assets:

The upward thrust of cryptocurrencies, such as Bitcoin and Ethereum, has delivered a new magnificence of digital property. While taken into consideration quite speculative, cryptocurrencies offer a decentralized and without borderlines opportunity investment.

Investors should method this option with warning because of its volatility and evolving regulatory panorama.

6. Art and Collectibles:

Investing in art, first-rate wine, rare coins, or different collectibles may be an alternative strategy. The fee of these belongings may additionally respect through the years, and they can provide diversification. However, those investments require information and studies, in addition to consideration of garage and maintenance charges.

7. Peer-to-Peer Lending:

Peer-to-peer lending platforms connect borrowers immediately with character lenders, bypassing traditional economic establishments. Investors can earn hobby by way of lending money to people or small agencies. This alternative choice lets in for portfolio diversification even as contributing to social lending.

8. Real Estate Crowdfunding:

Real property crowdfunding structures allow investors to pool their budget to spend money on real property tasks. This presents get entry to to real estate investments with lower capital requirements and permits for diversification throughout exceptional homes and locations.

9. Structured Products:

Structured products are financial units created by combining numerous derivatives. These products can provide tailor-made threat-go back profiles and might consist of functions inclusive of predominant protection or participation in market profits. However, knowledge the complexity of those products is crucial earlier than investing.

10. Environmental, Social, and Governance (ESG) Investments:

- ESG investments recognition on companies that adhere to environmental, social, and governance ideas. These investments intention to generate superb social and environmental impacts whilst turning in financial returns. ESG finances and sustainable investments have received popularity amongst buyers seeking socially accountable options.

11. Collective Investment Schemes:

- Collective funding schemes, consisting of mutual budget and exchange-traded price range (ETFs), offer investors with a varied portfolio managed via professional fund managers. These budget can consciousness on diverse asset training, areas, or investment topics.

When considering alternative investments, it's important to behavior thorough research, apprehend the related risks, and align choices with man or woman financial dreams and chance tolerance. Diversifying across special asset classes can contribute to a well-balanced and resilient investment portfolio.

Chapter 6:

Mastering the Art of Negotiation and Income Growth

In the world of economic mastery, the talent of negotiation emerges as a powerful device for unlocking income increase and achieving greater monetary success. The capability to barter efficiently extends beyond revenue discussions; it permeates diverse components of private and professional life, influencing earnings, funding deals, or even each day expenses.

This bankruptcy delves into the artwork of negotiation, offering insights into strategies which could elevate one's earning potential. From revenue negotiations in the place of business to securing favorable terms in enterprise transactions, getting to know negotiation strategies becomes a cornerstone for economic empowerment.

Readers will explore the psychology of negotiation, information the importance of guidance, active listening, and strategic communication. Uncovering the nuances of win-win eventualities, this bankruptcy courses people on a way to create collectively beneficial outcomes that propel income growth and monetary stability.

Furthermore, the bankruptcy addresses the significance of negotiating costs, from application bills to fundamental purchases, equipping readers with the talents to optimize their economic outflows. By honing negotiation prowess, individuals can navigate economic landscapes with self assurance, ensuring that every financial transaction becomes an opportunity for earnings enhancement.

Ultimately, "Mastering the Art of Negotiation and Income Growth" empowers readers to method negotiations as strategic endeavors, fostering a mindset that transforms each monetary interplay into a stepping stone closer to more prosperity. As negotiations become an crucial a part of the monetary toolkit, readers will discover themselves properly-located to harness income increase possibilities and navigate the monetary journey with talent and confidence.

6.1 Negotiating Your Way to a Higher Income

Negotiation is an art that transcends the confines of boardrooms and salary discussions, becoming a pivotal skill for those on the path to financial mastery. "Negotiating Your Way to a Higher Income" explores the nuanced world of negotiations, offering readers a comprehensive guide to elevating their earning potential.

This chapter delves into the intricacies of salary negotiations, providing strategies to navigate conversations with employers confidently. From initial job offers to performance reviews, readers will gain insights into articulating their value, showcasing achievements, and ultimately securing a remuneration that aligns with their worth.

Beyond the workplace, the chapter expands its focus to encompass various aspects of personal finance. It sheds light on negotiating better terms in business transactions, investments, and even day-to-day expenditures. By mastering the psychology of negotiation, readers learn to craft win-win scenarios that foster income growth and financial empowerment.

Preparation becomes a cornerstone of effective negotiation, with the chapter guiding readers on researching market standards, understanding their own financial goals, and developing persuasive communication skills. The art of active listening and the ability to create mutually beneficial outcomes are unveiled as indispensable tools for successful negotiation.

In "Negotiating Your Way to a Higher Income," readers are not only equipped with the skills to navigate salary discussions but are also empowered to approach various financial transactions with a strategic mindset. As negotiations transform into opportunities for income enhancement, individuals embark on a journey where financial empowerment is not just a goal but a skill refined through the art of negotiation.

Strategies for negotiating salary and benefits

Negotiating salary and benefits is a critical skill in the pursuit of financial empowerment. Whether entering a new job, seeking a promotion, or navigating a performance review, employing effective negotiation strategies is paramount. Here are key strategies to master the art of negotiating a favorable compensation package:

1. Research and Preparation:

Thoroughly research industry salary standards and benchmarks for the specific role and location. Armed with this information, develop a clear understanding of your market value. Consider factors such as experience, skills, and industry demand.

2. Know Your Worth:

Recognize and confidently communicate your professional achievements, skills, and unique contributions. Articulate how your qualifications align with the demands of the position and the value you bring to the organization.

3. Timing is Key:

Choose the right timing for negotiations. Ideally, discussions about salary and benefits should commence after a job offer has been extended but before it's accepted. This timing provides a window for constructive dialogue.

4. Be Open and Transparent:

Establish open communication with the employer. Clearly express your expectations and priorities regarding salary, benefits, and any additional perks. Transparency fosters a collaborative atmosphere and sets the stage for a mutually beneficial outcome.

5. Consider the Entire Package:

Salary is just one component of the compensation package. Evaluate the entire offering, including benefits such as health insurance, retirement plans, stock options, and bonuses. Sometimes, enhancing one aspect compensates for a lower salary.

6. Practice Effective Communication:

Hone your communication skills to express your needs and expectations clearly. Use confident and assertive language while maintaining a positive and collaborative tone. Listening actively to the employer's perspective is equally important.

7. Have a Range, Not a Fixed Number:

Instead of presenting a fixed number, offer a salary range based on your research. This provides flexibility and demonstrates your openness to negotiation. The range should reflect the lowest acceptable salary to the ideal compensation you seek.

8. Be Prepared to Justify Requests:

Anticipate potential questions or concerns from the employer and be ready to justify your requests. Provide examples of your accomplishments, the impact of your work, and how your skills align with the organization's goals.

9. Consider Non-Monetary Perks:

If salary negotiations reach an impasse, explore non-monetary perks such as flexible work arrangements, additional vacation days, professional development opportunities, or remote work options. These perks can enhance the overall package.

10. Know When to Compromise:

- While aiming for the best possible outcome, recognize when to compromise. Finding a middle ground that satisfies both parties is often the key to a successful negotiation. Be flexible and prioritize your long-term career goals.

Mastering the art of negotiating salary and benefits is a continuous process that evolves throughout one's career. By employing these strategies, individuals can navigate negotiations with confidence, ensuring that their compensation aligns with their skills, contributions, and overall career aspirations.

Leveraging skills for career advancement

In the dynamic landscape of professional growth, the ability to leverage skills becomes a cornerstone for navigating the trajectory of one's career. "Leveraging Skills for Career Advancement" is a chapter dedicated to unraveling the intricacies of skill utilization, offering insights that empower individuals to propel their careers forward.

This chapter delves into the strategic deployment of skills to achieve career milestones. It explores how a nuanced understanding of one's strengths and competencies can be harnessed to unlock opportunities for advancement. Rather than a passive accumulation of skills, readers are guided to actively leverage these assets as dynamic tools in their professional toolkit.

From technical proficiencies to soft skills like communication and leadership, the chapter underscores the importance of aligning skill sets with organizational objectives. It explores how proactive skill development, continuous learning, and staying abreast of industry trends position individuals as invaluable contributors within their respective fields.

Moreover, the chapter extends its focus beyond individual skill sets to encompass the art of collaboration. It explores how fostering a culture of knowledge sharing and mentorship within a professional ecosystem can amplify the impact of collective skills, creating a workplace environment conducive to innovation and growth.

"Leveraging Skills for Career Advancement" is not merely a discourse on personal development; it is a strategic guide for readers to mold their career trajectories actively. By mastering the art of skill utilization, individuals are empowered to not only advance within their current roles but also to navigate the evolving landscapes of their chosen industries. As the chapter unfolds, readers discover that the true essence of career advancement lies not just in acquiring skills but in strategically leveraging them to carve a path towards professional success and fulfillment.

6.2 Entrepreneurial Ventures for Income Growth

Embarking on entrepreneurial ventures is a transformative journey that holds the potential to redefine one's economic landscape. "Entrepreneurial Ventures for Income Growth" explores the dynamic realm of entrepreneurship, offering a comprehensive perspective on how people can leverage their creativity, skills, and determination to now not best generate income but also foster lengthy-term economic prosperity.

This chapter delves into the multifaceted aspects of entrepreneurship, beginning with the identification of opportunities. It encourages readers to discern gaps in the market, explore unmet needs, and conceive innovative answers. By cultivating an entrepreneurial mindset, people can liberate the door to income growth through the creation of merchandise, services, or answers that resonate with the market.

Strategic making plans is unveiled as a cornerstone of successful entrepreneurial ventures. The chapter guides readers on a way to develop a business plan, set clear objectives, and create a roadmap for implementation. This planning phase lays the basis for sustainable income boom and mitigates potential risks associated with venturing into the business world.

Furthermore, the chapter explores the significance of adaptability in the entrepreneurial landscape. Given the dynamic nature of markets, the ability to pivot, innovate, and embrace change becomes paramount. Entrepreneurs are encouraged to view challenges as opportunities for boom, learning, and refinement of their ventures.

The dialogue extends beyond the preliminary stages of entrepreneurship to address essential elements of business management. Readers advantage insights into effective marketing strategies, monetary management, and the establishment of a strong brand presence. These elements collectively contribute to income increase and the lengthy-term viability of entrepreneurial endeavors.

Collaboration and networking emerge as important components in the entrepreneurial journey. Building meaningful connections, seeking mentorship, and fostering partnerships contribute to a supportive ecosystem that fuels business growth. The chapter emphasizes the value of learning from experienced entrepreneurs and leveraging collective knowledge to navigate the complexities of entrepreneurship.

In "Entrepreneurial Ventures for Income Growth," readers are not most effective equipped with the principles of entrepreneurship but are inspired to take actionable steps closer to realizing their business ideas. The entrepreneurial journey, as depicted in this chapter, is not merely a pursuit of monetary gains; it is a transformative experience that empowers people to contribute to the economy, create value, and chart their own course in the direction of sustained income boom.

As the entrepreneurial spirit is ignited, readers are encouraged to view challenges as stepping stones, innovation as a riding force, and their ventures as vehicles for no longer only income boom but also personal fulfillment and professional effect.

Exploring entrepreneurial opportunities

The journey into entrepreneurship begins with the exploration of opportunities, a process that involves discerning needs, identifying gaps in the market, and envisioning innovative answers. "Exploring Entrepreneurial Opportunities" serves as a compass for individuals seeking to navigate this dynamic landscape, offering insights into the foundational steps that precede the creation of a successful entrepreneurial venture.

At the heart of entrepreneurial exploration is the cultivation of an innovative mindset. Recognizing that opportunities often arise from challenges or unmet needs, aspiring entrepreneurs are encouraged to view problems as catalysts for inventive answers. This mindset shift sets the stage for the identification of viable opportunities that align with the entrepreneur's abilties, interests, and the evolving demands of the market.

The chapter unfolds the importance of market research as a pivotal device for opportunity exploration. By delving into market dynamics, understanding consumer behaviors, and reading enterprise trends, entrepreneurs gain a comprehensive understanding of the landscape wherein their ventures will operate. This informed method permits for the identification of niches, target audiences, and potential areas for disruption.

Entrepreneurs are prompted to leverage their personal experiences and passions in the course of the exploration phase. Identifying opportunities that resonate personally increases the likelihood of sustained commitment and enthusiasm in the course of the entrepreneurial journey. The chapter underscores the power of aligning one's aspirations with market needs, creating a harmonious convergence that forms the foundation of a successful venture.

Strategic wondering becomes integral to possibility exploration. Aspiring entrepreneurs are guided to evaluate the scalability, feasibility, and uniqueness of their ideas. This involves assessing the competition, understanding potential challenges, and envisioning the lengthy-term sustainability of the proposed venture. A well-idea-out strategy at this stage lays the basis for effective business making plans and implementation.

Building and scaling a side business for additional income

The concept of constructing and scaling a side business has evolved from a supplementary income source to a strategic avenue for economic empowerment. "Building and Scaling a Side Business for Additional Income" serves as a guide for people looking to harness their entrepreneurial spirit while retaining the balance of their primary income streams.

The chapter opens with the recognition that a side business isn't always merely a pursuit of extra income; it's far a deliberate effort to create a sustainable venture that complements one's abilities, interests, and monetary dreams. It encourages people to identify a niche or ardour that aligns with market demands, paving the manner for a side business that holds each personal and financial significance.

Strategic planning becomes a focus as the chapter unfolds. Entrepreneurs are guided to delineate clear objectives, define their target audience, and craft a unique value proposition. This foundational planning not simplest ensures the viability of the side business but also serves as a roadmap for its increase and scalability over time.

One of the key aspects emphasized is the importance of leveraging existing competencies and networks. Building a side business that aligns with one's expertise no longer only accelerates the preliminary setup however additionally facilitates a smoother route to scaling. The chapter encourages individuals to tap into their professional networks, drawing on relationships and experiences that contribute to the credibility and success of the venture.

As the side business gains traction, scalability becomes a central theme. Entrepreneurs are prompted to explore avenues for expansion, whether through product diversification, reaching new customer segments, or exploring complementary services. The chapter underscores the significance of adopting scalable business models that could accommodate boom without overwhelming resources.

The concept of scalability is further extended to the usage of technology and digital systems. Embracing online channels no longer handiest widens the reach of the side business but additionally streamlines operational processes. Whether via e-commerce, social media marketing, or virtual communication equipment, technology becomes an enabler for entrepreneurs seeking to scale their ventures efficiently.

Moreover, the chapter addresses the importance of time management and balance. Recognizing that a side business is often managed alongside other commitments, people are guided on how to prioritize duties, set realistic goals, and preserve a healthy work-life-business balance. This holistic method ensures that the side business enhances overall well-being rather than becoming a source of stress.

In essence, "Building and Scaling a Side Business for Additional Income" paints a comprehensive picture of the entrepreneurial journey. It recognizes that a side business is not confined to a temporary endeavor but has the potential to evolve into a thriving and sustainable income stream. As people embark on this entrepreneurial venture, the chapter serves as a compass, guiding them through the stages of creation, growth, and scalability, ultimately contributing to the realization of economic dreams and aspirations.

Chapter 7:

Tax Planning for Wealth Preservation

In the intricate realm of financial management, the seventh chapter delves into the crucial domain of "Tax Planning for Wealth Preservation." As taxes play a pivotal role in shaping the financial landscape, this chapter serves as a guide for individuals seeking strategic approaches to minimize tax liabilities and safeguard their accumulated wealth.

The chapter unfolds with an exploration of the fundamental principles of tax planning. It illuminates the significance of understanding tax laws, exemptions, and deductions as foundational elements in devising effective tax strategies. Readers are empowered to navigate the complexities of tax codes, ensuring compliance while optimizing their financial positions.

A central theme of the chapter revolves around proactive tax planning as a means of preserving wealth. It delves into the various avenues available to individuals, from maximizing deductions and credits to strategically timing financial transactions. By aligning financial decisions with tax implications, readers learn to minimize their tax burdens and enhance overall wealth retention.

Moreover, the chapter underscores the importance of staying informed about changes in tax legislation. As tax laws evolve, so should the strategies employed for wealth preservation.

Readers are guided on how to stay abreast of tax reforms and adapt their planning accordingly, ensuring continued efficacy in safeguarding their financial resources.

The holistic approach to tax planning extends beyond individual income to encompass investments, estates, and long-term financial goals. The chapter illuminates the interplay between different financial elements and tax considerations, providing readers with a comprehensive understanding of how strategic planning can fortify their wealth against unnecessary erosion.

In essence, "Tax Planning for Wealth Preservation" is not merely a guide to complying with tax obligations; it is a strategic roadmap for individuals to proactively navigate the tax landscape in a way that aligns with their broader financial objectives. As the chapter unfolds, readers are equipped with insights and tools to craft tax strategies that not only preserve their wealth but also contribute to the realization of their long-term financial aspirations.

7.1 Understanding the Basics of Tax Planning

In the financial journey towards wealth preservation, a foundational aspect is unraveling the intricacies of tax planning. "Understanding the Basics of Tax Planning" is a comprehensive exploration into the fundamental principles that underpin effective tax strategies, empowering individuals to navigate the complexities of the tax landscape with intentionality and foresight.

At its core, tax planning involves the strategic organization of one's financial affairs to minimize tax liabilities. This chapter begins by illuminating the importance of grasping the tax laws and regulations that govern personal finances. By developing a foundational understanding of tax codes, exemptions, and deductions, individuals can proactively shape their financial decisions to align with optimal tax outcomes.

The chapter unfolds with an emphasis on the proactive nature of tax planning. Rather than viewing taxes as an inevitable burden, individuals are encouraged to approach them as variables within their control. By strategically timing financial transactions, maximizing eligible deductions, and leveraging available tax credits, individuals can actively shape their tax obligations in a manner that preserves and enhances their wealth.

Central to effective tax planning is the principle of compliance. Understanding the legal framework within which taxes operate ensures that individuals not only optimize their financial positions but also remain within the bounds of the law. This compliance-oriented approach provides a solid foundation for sustainable and responsible tax planning strategies.

The chapter extends beyond the immediate scope of income taxes to encompass a holistic view of financial planning. It explores how tax considerations permeate various aspects of personal finance, including investments, estates, and retirement planning. Readers gain insights into the symbiotic relationship between financial decisions and their tax implications, fostering a nuanced understanding of the broader impact of tax planning on wealth preservation.

As the financial landscape continually evolves, the chapter underscores the importance of staying informed about changes in tax legislation. Tax laws are dynamic, and an effective tax planning strategy adapts to these changes. Readers are guided on how to cultivate a proactive approach to staying abreast of tax reforms, ensuring that their tax planning remains responsive and aligned with their financial goals.

In essence, "Understanding the Basics of Tax Planning" demystifies the seemingly complex world of taxes, empowering individuals to approach tax planning with clarity and purpose. By grasping the foundational principles, cultivating a proactive mindset, and recognizing the interconnectedness of financial decisions and tax implications, readers are equipped to embark on a journey of strategic tax planning that contributes to the preservation and growth of their wealth.

Maximizing tax advantages

In the intricate tapestry of personal finance, the art of maximizing tax advantages emerges as a strategic cornerstone for individuals seeking to preserve and enhance their wealth. This chapter, "Maximizing Tax Advantages," unveils the various avenues through which individuals can navigate the tax landscape with acumen, optimizing their financial positions while ensuring compliance with relevant laws.

At its essence, maximizing tax advantages involves a proactive approach to organizing one's financial affairs to leverage available deductions, exemptions, and credits. The chapter opens with an exploration of the myriad deductions that individuals can harness to reduce their taxable income. From business expenses to educational costs and homeownership-related deductions, readers gain insights into the diverse array of opportunities for minimizing tax burdens.

The concept of tax credits takes center stage as a powerful tool for maximizing tax advantages. Unlike deductions that reduce taxable income, credits directly reduce the amount of tax owed. The chapter delves into various tax credits, including those for education, energy efficiency, and child care, guiding readers on how to capitalize on these credits to optimize their overall tax liability.

Strategic timing of financial transactions is unveiled as another key element in maximizing tax advantages. The chapter explores how individuals can leverage the timing of income recognition, capital gains realization, and charitable contributions to their advantage. By aligning financial decisions with the ebb and flow of the tax calendar, individuals can strategically minimize their tax liabilities.

Moreover, the chapter emphasizes the importance of retirement planning in the context of tax advantages. Contributions to retirement accounts not only secure financial futures but also offer immediate tax benefits. Readers are guided on how to navigate the landscape of retirement accounts, such as 401(k)s and IRAs, to maximize their tax advantages while building a robust nest egg.

The entrepreneurial spirit is also acknowledged as a realm ripe for tax optimization. Business owners are introduced to various strategies, from selecting the right business structure to capitalizing on deductions available to entrepreneurs. By understanding the intersection of business decisions and tax implications, individuals embarking on entrepreneurial ventures can proactively position themselves for maximum tax advantages.

As the chapter unfolds, a recurrent theme is the dynamic nature of tax laws. Maximizing tax advantages requires a continuous commitment to staying informed about changes in legislation. Readers are empowered to cultivate a proactive approach to tax planning, ensuring that their strategies remain responsive to the evolving tax landscape.

In essence, "Maximizing Tax Advantages" is not just a guide to minimizing tax liabilities; it is an invitation to view the tax landscape as a canvas of opportunities. By approaching tax planning with strategic foresight, individuals can proactively shape their financial destinies, harnessing the available advantages to not only preserve but also grow their wealth.

Reducing tax liabilities through strategic planning

In the intricate dance of personal finance, the chapter "Reducing Tax Liabilities through Strategic Planning" unfolds as a strategic guide for individuals seeking to navigate the labyrinth of tax obligations with finesse. It delves into the art of proactive planning, offering insights into how individuals can strategically shape their financial decisions to minimize tax liabilities while remaining in compliance with existing tax laws.

At its core, the chapter illuminates the principle that reducing tax liabilities is not merely a reactive measure but a deliberate and strategic undertaking. It commences with an exploration of the importance of understanding the tax code. By unraveling the intricacies of tax laws, individuals can identify opportunities to optimize their financial decisions, ensuring that every action aligns with the overarching goal of reducing tax burdens.

Strategic planning involves a nuanced understanding of deductions, exemptions, and credits available within the tax framework. The chapter guides readers through various deductions, including those related to education, homeownership, and charitable contributions. By strategically incorporating these elements into their financial decisions, individuals can chip away at their taxable income, ultimately reducing their overall tax liabilities.

Timing emerges as a crucial component in the strategic reduction of tax liabilities. The chapter explores how individuals can strategically time their financial transactions to capitalize on tax advantages. Whether it's recognizing income, realizing capital gains, or making charitable contributions, the timing of these actions can significantly impact the amount owed in taxes. By aligning financial decisions with the ebb and flow of the tax calendar, individuals can optimize their tax positions.

Moreover, the chapter underscores the role of retirement planning in tax reduction. Contributions to retirement accounts not only secure financial futures but also offer immediate tax benefits. The strategic allocation of funds to retirement vehicles, such as 401(k)s or IRAs, becomes a key aspect of reducing current tax liabilities while building a robust financial foundation for the future.

Entrepreneurs are also invited to explore the realm of tax reduction through strategic planning. The chapter unveils various strategies for business owners, from selecting tax-efficient business structures to navigating deductions and credits available to entrepreneurs. By integrating tax considerations into their business decisions, entrepreneurs can proactively position themselves for reduced tax liabilities.

As the chapter unfolds, it highlights the dynamic nature of tax laws and the necessity of staying informed about changes in legislation. The proactive approach to tax planning is not a one-time endeavor but an ongoing commitment to adapting strategies in response to shifts in the tax landscape.

In essence, "Reducing Tax Liabilities through Strategic Planning" is not just a manual for compliance; it is an invitation to view taxes as a canvas for strategic decision-making. By navigating the intricacies of the tax landscape with intentionality and foresight, individuals can craft a financial narrative that not only complies with tax laws but strategically reduces tax liabilities, contributing to the preservation and growth of their overall wealth.

7.2 Wealth Preservation Strategies

In the intricate dance of personal finance, the chapter "Reducing Tax Liabilities through Strategic Planning" unfolds as a strategic guide for individuals seeking to navigate the labyrinth of tax obligations with finesse. It delves into the art of proactive planning, offering insights into how individuals can strategically shape their financial decisions to minimize tax liabilities while remaining in compliance with existing tax laws.

At its core, the chapter illuminates the principle that reducing tax liabilities is not merely a reactive measure but a deliberate and strategic undertaking. It commences with an exploration of the importance of understanding the tax code. By unraveling the intricacies of tax laws, individuals can identify opportunities to optimize their financial decisions, ensuring that every action aligns with the overarching goal of reducing tax burdens.

Strategic planning involves a nuanced understanding of deductions, exemptions, and credits available within the tax framework. The chapter guides readers through various deductions, including those related to education, homeownership, and charitable contributions. By strategically incorporating these elements into their financial decisions, individuals can chip away at their taxable income, ultimately reducing their overall tax liabilities.

Timing emerges as a crucial component in the strategic reduction of tax liabilities. The chapter explores how individuals can strategically time their financial transactions to capitalize on tax advantages. Whether it's recognizing income, realizing capital gains, or making charitable contributions, the timing of these actions can significantly impact the amount owed in taxes. By aligning financial decisions with the ebb and flow of the tax calendar, individuals can optimize their tax positions.

Moreover, the chapter underscores the role of retirement planning in tax reduction. Contributions to retirement accounts not only secure financial futures but also offer immediate tax benefits. The strategic allocation of funds to retirement vehicles, such as 401(k)s or IRAs, becomes a key aspect of reducing current tax liabilities while building a robust financial foundation for the future.

Entrepreneurs are also invited to explore the realm of tax reduction through strategic planning. The chapter unveils various strategies for business owners, from selecting tax-efficient business structures to navigating deductions and credits available to entrepreneurs. By integrating tax considerations into their business decisions, entrepreneurs can proactively position themselves for reduced tax liabilities.

As the chapter unfolds, it highlights the dynamic nature of tax laws and the necessity of staying informed about changes in legislation. The proactive approach to tax planning is not a one-time endeavor but an ongoing commitment to adapting strategies in response to shifts in the tax landscape.

In essence, "Reducing Tax Liabilities through Strategic Planning" is not just a manual for compliance; it is an invitation to view taxes as a canvas for strategic decision-making. By navigating the intricacies of the tax landscape with intentionality and foresight, individuals can craft a financial narrative that not only complies with tax laws but strategically reduces tax liabilities, contributing to the preservation and growth of their overall wealth.

Estate planning and legacy building

In the complicated journey of private finance, "Estate Planning and Building a Legacy" emerges as a cornerstone that invites people to mirror on the lasting effect in their monetary selections throughout generations. Beyond the realm of wealth accumulation, this bankruptcy delves into the artwork of creating a legacy—a story about values, aspirations, and economic stewardship that spans an entire life.

In essence, estate-making plans aren't only a felony necessity, but a profound act of intentionality. It involves cautious orchestration of one's belongings to ensure that it's far transferred easily and in accordance with one's wishes. This chapter develops the significance of viewing property-making plans as a strategic endeavour that goes past wealth distribution—it is the carving of a legacy that displays private values and family aspirations.

Wills and trusts are emerging as ancillary equipment in the estate planning toolbox. Through the strategic use of felony equipment, people can dictate how their property is disbursed, minimizing tax effects and ensuring an easy transition of wealth. This bankruptcy illuminates the significance of reconciling the complexities of property-making plans with broader financial desires, making it simpler to create a legacy that stands the check of time.

Legacy building, within the context of property-making plans, is a tale intentionally created to pass on values and principles to destiny generations. This bankruptcy looks at how people can imbue their property plans with a feel of reason that reflects no longer most effectively the fabric wealth they've amassed, but additionally the ethos and beliefs that outline their legacy. This intentional approach transforms estate-making plans from a procedural exercise into a profound act of family and personal storytelling.

In addition, the bankruptcy highlights the significance of verbal exchange in the family as an imperative factor in estate-making plans and legacy building. Transparent and open speaking about economic values, aspirations and justification of specific decisions promotes information and unity among family participants. It permits people to specify their intentions, mitigates potential conflicts, and ensures that their family concord is maintained.

Beyond an instantaneous circle of relatives, legacy construction extends to philanthropy and community impact. This chapter explores how people can incorporate charitable giving into their property plans to create a legacy of social duty and contribution. Whether through the status quo of charitable trusts, foundations or strategic philanthropic initiatives, individuals can imprint their values into the broader tapestry of society.

Heritage construction, as discussed in this chapter, is a dynamic and ongoing process. It acknowledges that values, aspirations and economic environments evolve. Individuals are consequently encouraged to review and adapt their estate plans to reflect changing instances and ensure that their legacies remain relevant and impactful.

"Estate Planning and Legacy Building" is essentially an invitation to transcend the traditional view of wealth control. It encourages people to now not only acquire wealth but also to deliberately form the tale of their monetary legacy. As the chapter unfolds, readers are encouraged to reflect on consideration of the lasting effect of their financial decisions, viewing property planning no longer as a procedural mission but as a profound and functional act of building a long-lasting legacy.

Ensuring financial security for future generations

In the complex tapestry of private finance, the bankruptcy on "Ensuring Financial Security for Future Generations" unfolds as a testomony to the profound responsibility individuals endure in shaping the monetary destinies of people who observe. This narrative transcends the conventional information of accumulating wealth for oneself; it's miles an intentional and strategic commitment to safeguarding the financial well-being of future generations.

At its middle, ensuring financial protection for destiny generations involves a holistic and farsighted method to wealth management. It goes past the instant worries of every day financial choices to embody deliberate and strategic movements that pave the way for sustained prosperity. The bankruptcy opens with the popularity that the impact of those choices extends a long way past an character's lifetime, creating a legacy that echoes thru the corridors of time.

Estate making plans surfaces as a relevant theme within the quest for making sure monetary security across generations. The chapter delves into the strategic usage of criminal units consisting of wills and trusts, supplying people a roadmap to navigate the complex terrain of asset distribution. By meticulously crafting an property plan, people can make sure the seamless transfer of wealth to heirs, minimizing tax implications and mitigating potential conflicts.

Moreover, the chapter invitations readers to view property planning no longer simply as a criminal exercising but as an intentional act of legacy building. Beyond the monetary property, people are endorsed to impart values, standards, and aspirations to destiny generations. This intentional transmission of information ensures that the actual essence of wealth—beyond its fabric shape—is preserved and surpassed on.

Strategic wealth management becomes a crucial factor of ensuring economic protection. The bankruptcy unfolds the significance of investment diversification, risk management, and disciplined economic behavior. By adopting a multifaceted approach to wealth accumulation and preservation, people can weather the inevitable fluctuations in financial markets, laying the basis for sustained monetary security for their progeny.

Education making plans emerges as any other essential aspect in the narrative of ensuring economic protection for destiny generations. The bankruptcy explores techniques for investment instructional endeavors, whether or not via devoted financial savings money owed, trusts, or other financial devices. By proactively addressing the charges of education, people make contributions to the empowerment of future generations, ensuring get admission to to opportunities that transcend economic limitations.

Communication in the circle of relatives emerges as a topic intertwined with the cloth of economic safety. The bankruptcy underscores the importance of open and transparent talk about monetary subjects. By fostering an environment wherein circle of relatives participants can talk values, aspirations, and financial decisions, individuals contribute to a shared information that fortifies the familial foundation.

Philanthropy becomes a poignant element within the narrative of ensuring economic protection for destiny generations. The chapter explores how individuals can incorporate charitable giving into their wealth management strategy, fostering a feel of social duty and community impact. By contributing to causes aligned with family values, people not handiest leave a monetary legacy but additionally a legacy of compassion and contribution.

In essence, "Ensuring Financial Security for Future Generations" beckons individuals to transcend the ephemeral nature of monetary decisions. It is an invite to planned on the iconic impact of selections and moves, recognizing that the authentic measure of monetary achievement lies not simply inside the accumulation of wealth however within the intentional and strategic efforts to stable the economic properly-being of generations but to return. As the chapter unfolds, readers are brought about to view their economic journey as a legacy-building enterprise—an intentional and functional contribution to the prosperity of destiny circle of relatives traces.

Chapter 8:

Mindful Spending and Lifestyle Design

In the problematic dance of financial mastery, "Chapter 8: Mindful Spending and Lifestyle Design" invites people to a paradigm shift in their approach to cash. This bankruptcy unfolds as a transformative manual, urging readers to include the philosophy of aware spending and intentional life-style layout. Far beyond conventional notions of budgeting, it explores the profound effect of aware economic selections on each on the spot well-being and lengthy-time period achievement.

At its essence, mindful spending transcends the limitations of mere fee monitoring. It is a deliberate and considerate method to monetary choices, considering no longer just the instantaneous application of a purchase but its alignment with non-public values and aspirations. The chapter illuminates the idea that each monetary desire is a mirrored image of one's priorities and, whilst approached mindfully, turns into a tool for sculpting a life in harmony with one's truest desires.

Lifestyle layout, intricately woven into this bankruptcy, is a call to intentional living. It urges readers to architect a lifestyles that aligns with their middle values and lengthy-time period desires. The chapter navigates the terrain of intentional alternatives, prompting readers to impeach societal norms and domesticate a way of life that fosters real happiness and success.

Moreover, the bankruptcy delves into the psychology of spending, exploring how purchaser choices are regularly stimulated via societal expectations and external pressures. By fostering attention around those influences, readers advantage the equipment to make financial selections that aren't dictated by way of external forces but are grounded in a deep know-how of personal values.

Mindful spending isn't about deprivation; it's far approximately cultivating a experience of abundance thru aware alternatives. The bankruptcy publications readers on how to distinguish among want and desires, encouraging a shift in the direction of studies and investments that contribute to lengthy-time period properly-being as opposed to non permanent gratification.

As the bankruptcy unfolds, life-style design emerges as a powerful device for financial empowerment. It prompts readers to assess their present day existence, become aware of areas of misalignment, and deliberately craft a lifestyles that displays their particular aspirations. By shedding the burden of societal expectations, people can embark on a adventure of intentional living that aligns with their financial desires.

In essence, "Chapter 8: Mindful Spending and Lifestyle Design" is an ode to the transformative capacity of aware financial selections. It beckons readers to embark on a adventure of self-discovery, wondering societal norms, and deliberately crafting a existence that not handiest aligns with monetary dreams but also resonates with the genuine essence of personal success. As the bankruptcy unfolds, readers are inspired to view aware spending and way of life design no longer as constraints but as liberating gear for sculpting a lifestyles of motive, abundance, and enduring pleasure.

8.1 Cultivating Mindful Spending Habits

In the location of private finance, the cultivation of aware spending conduct emerges as a transformative adventure toward intentional and satisfying financial picks. Mindful spending goes beyond the conventional idea of budgeting; it includes a aware and deliberate approach to each financial selection, recognizing the profound effect every preference has on one's common properly-being and financial destiny.

At its center, cultivating aware spending behavior requires a heightened cognizance of the motivations and values that underpin financial alternatives. It prompts people to question the real necessity and alignment of every expenditure with their dreams and aspirations. This intentional inquiry transforms spending from a passive, routine act right into a conscious and useful selection-making system.

Mindful spending is anchored inside the principle of aligning monetary selections with personal values. It encourages people to reflect on what absolutely brings them satisfaction, achievement, and lengthy-term pleasure. By knowledge the deeper motivations at the back of spending, individuals may want to make selections that contribute undoubtedly to their not unusual well-being in preference to succumbing to impulsive or societal-driven consumption styles.

The workout of conscious spending includes distinguishing among needs and wants. It activates individuals to evaluate whether or now not a purchase is driven by way of the use of true necessity or if it is a fleeting choice brought on through method of out of doors pressures. This discernment permits individuals to channel assets toward what genuinely topics to them, fostering a experience of purpose and intentionality of their monetary lives.

Furthermore, cultivating conscious spending behavior includes breaking loose from societal expectations and consumerist norms. It encourages human beings to impeach the winning narrative that friends happiness with fabric accumulation. By consciously opting for reports, relationships, and investments that contribute to prolonged-time period nicely-being, humans can reshape their dating with coins and find out lasting fulfillment.

An essential element of cultivating conscious spending conduct is growing a holistic view of monetary well-being. It goes beyond the numbers on a stability sheet and encompasses the general effect of financial selections on mental, emotional, and bodily fitness. This holistic mind-set turns on human beings to recall the lengthy-term effects of their spending behavior and make picks that contribute to sustained properly-being.

In essence, cultivating aware spending behavior is a journey of self-discovery and intentional living. It is ready reclaiming control over one's monetary narrative, aligning spending options with personal values, and fostering a feel of abundance thru aware choices. As human beings embark in this transformative adventure, they no longer only shape a greater strong monetary destiny but also cultivate a existence that resonates with authenticity, cause, and enduring pleasure.

Evaluating and optimizing spending patterns

In the pursuit of economic mastery, the ongoing process of comparing and optimizing spending styles stands as a key element in constructing a stable foundation for long-term financial well-being. This dynamic practice involves a non-stop and aware evaluation of ways financial assets are allocated, with the goal of maximizing cost, aligning with non-public priorities, and fostering sustainable monetary health.

At its core, comparing spending patterns calls for a complete and honest exam of man or woman prices. It prompts people to scrutinize their economic conduct, discerning between crucial wishes and discretionary wants. By gaining readability at the motivations at the back of each expenditure, people can perceive regions for optimization and reallocate sources toward what really topics to them.

Optimizing spending patterns entails a strategic and intentional reshaping of economic selections. It calls for individuals to impeach the effectiveness in their current spending behavior in achieving their broader economic desires. This procedure is not about enforcing strict austerity measures but about ensuring that monetary sources are directed purposefully in the direction of priorities including financial savings, investments, and debt discount.

A important element of this assessment is the identification of useless or impulse-driven spending. By spotting and curtailing impulsive purchases, individuals can reclaim manipulate over their economic narrative. This may additionally involve putting spending limits, organising budgets, or leveraging technological tools that provide insights into spending patterns. The aim is to empower individuals to make knowledgeable and intentional picks aligned with their monetary goals.

Furthermore, optimizing spending styles involves a nuanced attention of life-style selections. It encourages individuals to assess whether or not present day spending aligns with their values and lengthy-term aspirations. This procedure may additionally entail reprioritizing expenses to mirror changing circumstances, shifting from cloth accumulation to reviews, or aligning spending with private goals which includes schooling, travel, or entrepreneurship.

The exercise of evaluating and optimizing spending styles extends beyond individual transactions to embody a holistic view of financial properly-being. It activates people to bear in mind the impact in their spending on average economic health, which include factors consisting of emergency fund contributions, debt discount, and long-term financial savings. This holistic angle ensures that monetary decisions make a contribution to both immediately pride and sustainable economic resilience.

In essence, the continuing journey of comparing and optimizing spending styles is a dynamic and empowering exercise. It empowers people to actively form their economic destinies, fostering a feel of manipulate, purpose, and intentionality of their monetary lives. As individuals have interaction in this continuous procedure of evaluation and adjustment, they now not handiest optimize their spending for fast satisfaction but additionally pave the way for a greater stable and pleasing monetary destiny.

Practicing conscious consumerism

On a global scale full of choices and options, conscious consumerism training is proving to be an effective and intentional method of purchasing. It goes beyond the transactional nature of purchasing goods and services and challenges people to create alternatives that align with their values, promote sustainability, and contribute to positive social and environmental impacts.

At its core, conscious consumerism involves a heightened awareness of the adventure a product experiences from production to consumption. It activates people to be mindful of the moral, environmental and social consequences of their purchases. The exercise is a departure from impulse or convenience shopping and encourages customers to be intentional stewards of their economic electricity.

One of the key aspects of conscious consumerism is supply chain control. Individuals are advised to find out approximately the origin and production processes of the goods they are purchasing. This consists of considerations along with true labor practices, ethical sourcing of materials and the environmental impact of production techniques. By helping products and agencies with clear and responsible practices, consumers become catalysts for fantastic business.

Another measure of conscious consumerism involves making choices that are consistent with private values. This can additionally consist of choosing goods that the guide believes in, consisting of true trade, environmental protection or social justice. By aligning purchasing decisions with values, individuals infuse intentionality into their patronage decisions, reshaping each transaction directly to advance aid for ideals they hold dear.

In addition, the conscious buyer takes into account the durability and sustainability of the products. Choosing tools with robustness and minimal impact on the environment contributes to reducing waste and leads to a more sustainable lifestyle. Additionally, this practice can include choosing products with recyclable packaging, helping brands that are committed to reducing their carbon footprint, or deciding on items that can be designed for durability instead of planned obsolescence.

Educating yourself about the goods and businesses you help is the foundation of being aware of consumerism. This includes getting to know brands, reading reviews and keeping up with industry practices. Armed with information, consumers are empowered to create alternatives that resonate with their values and contribute to broader dreams of sustainability and social responsibility.

In addition, conscious consumerism goes beyond tangible products to include offers and messages. It activates people to be mindful of the impact of their decisions on surrounding communities and global ecosystems. This can additionally include helping neighborhood groups, finding eco-friendly deals, or deciding on stories that favor cultural sensitivity and responsible tourism.

Conscious consumerism work is essentially a holistic and transformational technique for the act of purchasing. It allows individuals to use their purchasing power responsibly, promotes good exchange in industries and contributes to a extra moral and sustainable international market. As individuals embody this deliberate way of thinking, they act as energetic individuals in shaping an international environment in which customer alternatives are not just expressions of private preferences, but additionally impressive contributions to a fairer, sustainable, and just destiny.

8.2 Designing a Lifestyle Aligned with Financial Freedom

In the pursuit of financial freedom, the intentional act of designing a lifestyle turns into a pivotal and empowering endeavor. This intentional method transcends conventional notions of life to create a harmonious and functional existence that aligns seamlessly with the overarching goal of achieving and maintaining financial freedom.

At its core, designing a lifestyle for financial freedom involves deep self-evaluation and clear imagination and clairvoyance of what approach to financial freedom approaches for that person. It's a departure from traditional expectations and societal norms and encourages people to create an existence that resonates with their particular values, aspirations and long-term financial goals.

The process begins with a complete understanding of economic dreams 1. This includes defining a preferred level of monetary independence, whether or not it is early retirement, the ability to pursue passion projects, or the freedom to travel extensively. Clarifying these goals serves as a celebrity guide to lifestyle organization and provides a blueprint for intentional decisions.

Central to this idea is the adoption of minimalism and conscious spending. Designing a lifestyle for economic freedom encourages individuals to examine their spending habits and prioritize experiences and possessions that contribute to long-term well-being. It involves distinguishing between wants and desires, promoting contentment with much less material accumulation, and channeling resources into investments and experiences that practically count.

Strategic career choices play a significant role in this way of life. Individuals are encouraged to combine their professional hobbies with private passions and values. This can also include exploring entrepreneurship, a career that gives everyone financial praise and success, or strategically using talents and knowledge to create income streams leading to monetary independence.

Financial training is becoming a lifestyle cornerstone for financial freedom. Individuals are empowered to recognize investment strategies, tax planning and principles of wealth creation. This know-how equips them to make informed decisions that move them closer to financial independence and resilience and shape a lifestyle where financial literacy is an integral part of everyday life.

Embracing frugality is another key detail. Now this does not mean sacrificing joy or forgoing pleasure, however as an alternative adopting a mindset of conscious spending and deliberate selection. It involves comparing whether or not each rate is in line with the overall goal of financial freedom and making decisions that contribute to long-term financial well-being.

Beyond economic concerns, arranging a lifestyle for economic freedom involves cultivating a holistic technique for well-being. This includes prioritizing physical and mental health, nurturing meaningful relationships, and fostering personal growth. A balanced and healthy life becomes the inspiration behind financial freedom, ensuring that the accumulation of wealth is not always a guide to itself, but a method to a satisfying and purposeful lifestyle.

In essence, designing a lifestyle aligned with monetary freedom is a transformative and intentional adventure. It is the conscious act of creating a lifestyle that exceeds society's expectations, aligns with private values, and enables individuals to legibly and purposefully embark on the path to financial independence. When individuals embark on this adventure, they are now not only reshaping their money dating, but in addition creating a life that harmonizes monetary prosperity with real fulfillment and lasting pleasure.

Balancing financial goals with lifestyle choices

Achieving a harmonious balance between monetary desires and lifestyle is a subtle and deliberate effort that requires thoughtful examination of values, aspirations, and the preferred trajectory of their economic adventure. This delicate balance involves aligning monetary goals with the way one chooses to live, ensuring that each choice contributes to each instant gratification and long-term monetary well-being.

Amidst the hanging balance between monetary desires and lifestyle alternatives, it involves a complete understanding of one's priorities. Individuals are encouraged to clarify their financial goals, whether it's debt relief, wealth accumulation, home ownership or early retirement. This clear bureaucracy is the foundation upon which lifestyle choices can be consciously made to guide those overarching financial aspirations.

One key consideration in this stability is the deliberate evaluation of spending habits. It includes the distinction between necessary expenses and discretionary fees, noting that every financial choice has an impact on the ability to obtain broader monetary goals. This control encourages people to make choices that align with their priorities and undoubtedly contribute to their economic journey.

The idea extends to the world of career choice. Individuals are advised to assess their professional activities in accordance with their lifestyle and financial aspirations. This may also include deciding on a career that offers stability between financial rewards and private accomplishments, making strategic use of abilities for entrepreneurial endeavors, or exploring flexible work arrangements that are consistent with lifestyle alternatives.

Additionally, balancing money goals and lifestyle requires a shift toward intentional spending. It encourages individuals to look at purchases that aren't exactly the most adept right now through the lens of immediate gratification, but additionally from the point of view of their long-term impact on economic goals. This can also include practicing mindful consumerism, prioritizing pleasure over quantity, and adopting a minimalist approach that encourages contentment with little.

The integration of economic education into everyday existence becomes a crucial detail of this stability. Individuals are empowered to continually learn about financing strategies, tax plans and wealth building concepts. This understanding equips them to make informed decisions that align with their financial goals, while allowing for lifestyle alternatives that contribute to a normal good life.

Balancing financial aspirations with lifestyle choices also requires recognizing that existence is dynamic and priorities can also shift. This requires individuals to regularly reassess their financial goals and adapt them to meet evolving lifestyle options, career aspirations and living standards. Flexibility and adaptability have become important ingredients for maintaining balance within in the face of conversion situations.

Achieving stability between monetary desires and lifestyle alternatives is essentially a continuous technique of self-mirror image and deliberate decision-making. It involves combining financial aspirations and the pursuit of a meaningful and fulfilling lifestyle. As people move through this sensitive dance, they cultivate a way of life that no longer aids economic well-being, but also resonates with authenticity, sanity, and lasting joy.

Making intentional decisions for a fulfilling life

Crafting a fulfilling life requires a deliberate and intentional approach to decision-making, where each choice contributes to a sense of purpose, satisfaction, and overall well-being. The essence of making intentional decisions lies in aligning actions with personal values, aspirations, and the pursuit of a life that resonates with authenticity and meaning.

At its core, intentional decision-making involves a profound self-awareness—a clear understanding of one's values, passions, and long-term goals. This self-awareness serves as the compass guiding decisions, ensuring that each choice is a conscious step toward a life that reflects one's truest self. It is a departure from reactive decision-making and a move toward proactively shaping one's destiny.

The process begins with a thoughtful examination of personal values. Individuals are encouraged to identify the principles and beliefs that are foundational to their identity. These values become the criteria against which decisions are measured, guiding individuals to make choices that align with their deeply held convictions and contribute to a sense of integrity and authenticity.

As individuals embark on the journey of intentional decision-making, they confront the need to prioritize. It involves acknowledging that time, energy, and resources are finite, necessitating choices that reflect genuine priorities. This may entail letting go of activities or commitments that do not align with overarching life goals, fostering a focused and purpose-driven existence.

Moreover, intentional decisions extend to the realm of relationships. Individuals are prompted to cultivate connections that nourish their well-being and contribute positively to their life journey. This may involve setting boundaries, surrounding oneself with supportive and like-minded individuals, and fostering relationships that align with the vision of a fulfilling life.

The concept of intentional decision-making intertwines with the pursuit of lifelong learning. Individuals are encouraged to seek knowledge, explore new experiences, and continuously evolve. This commitment to growth ensures that decisions are informed by a dynamic understanding of oneself and the ever-changing landscape of possibilities.

A crucial aspect of making intentional decisions is embracing a positive mindset. It involves cultivating gratitude, resilience, and a focus on the present moment. By adopting a positive outlook, individuals navigate challenges with grace, appreciate the richness of their experiences, and make decisions that contribute to a sense of joy and fulfillment.

In the financial realm, intentional decision-making takes the form of conscious spending and mindful financial choices. Individuals are empowered to make financial decisions that align with their values and long-term goals, whether it involves saving for specific milestones, investing in experiences, or contributing to causes that hold personal significance.

In essence, making intentional decisions for a fulfilling life is a transformative and ongoing process. It is about recognizing the power each decision holds in shaping the trajectory of one's life and deliberately choosing actions that contribute to a sense of purpose, authenticity, and joy. As individuals embrace this intentional mindset, they pave the way for a life that resonates with meaning, fulfillment, and the enduring satisfaction of having actively and purposefully shaped their own journey.

Chapter 9:

Overcoming Financial Challenges

In the intricate tapestry of economic freedom, Chapter 9 serves as a manual via the labyrinth of inevitable demanding situations which could get up on the direction to financial empowerment. "Overcoming Financial Challenges" is not just a chapter; it's miles a beacon illuminating the resilience and strategies required to navigate unexpected hurdles and emerge more potent on the other aspect.

The chapter begins by means of acknowledging that the adventure to economic freedom is seldom a linear ascent. It explores the commonplace challenges people may additionally face, from sudden expenses and monetary downturns to private setbacks that can disrupt even the most meticulously crafted monetary plans.

Central to this exploration is the subject matter of adaptability. Readers are advocated to cultivate a mindset that views demanding situations not as insurmountable barriers however as opportunities for increase and studying. By embracing adaptability, individuals can pivot in the face of monetary adversity, adjusting their techniques and redefining goals to align with the evolving circumstances.

A vast awareness is placed on resilience—the capacity to resist and rebound from economic setbacks. The bankruptcy delves into the psychological elements of resilience, presenting insights into constructing mental fortitude and retaining a wonderful outlook during difficult times. It explores coping mechanisms, stress control strategies, and the importance of searching for aid from each economic and emotional perspectives.

Moreover, "Overcoming Financial Challenges" underscores the importance of contingency planning. Readers are guided via the method of establishing emergency funds, insurance insurance, and contingency budgets. By getting ready for the surprising, individuals can mitigate the effect of monetary demanding situations and keep a experience of balance at some stage in turbulent times.

The bankruptcy does no longer shrink back from addressing the emotional toll of financial demanding situations. It explores the psychological effect of setbacks, providing steering on handling stress, anxiety, and the emotional aspects of financial adversity. By acknowledging and addressing those emotional dimensions, readers are ready to navigate challenges with a holistic approach that considers both financial and intellectual well-being.

Ultimately, "Overcoming Financial Challenges" is a testament to the resilience inherent in the pursuit of financial freedom. It paints a practical photo of the adventure, acknowledging that setbacks are a herbal a part of the process. By providing realistic strategies, psychological insights, and a roadmap for building resilience, the chapter empowers readers to face challenges head-on and emerge from adversity with newfound energy and a deeper expertise of their own financial skills.

9.1 Navigating Economic Downturns

In the ever-shifting landscape of personal finance, the "Navigating the Economic Downturn" chapter is an essential compass to guide individuals through the complexities of financial turmoil. Economic downturns are inherent in the cyclical nature of economies, and this chapter serves as a strategic guide to help readers who are now not the most adept at weathering the storm but also thriving in the face of economic

The chapter opens with a sober acknowledgment of the uncertainties and disruptions that accompany economic downturns. He emphasizes that preparedness is the cornerstone of resilience. Readers are advised to assess their current financial position, identify vulnerabilities and strengthen their financial foundations to withstand the effects of economic contractions.

Central to navigating economic downturns is a realistic budgeting method. The chapter offers sound insights into recession-proof budgeting, emphasizing the importance of distinguishing between material and non-material expenditures. It guides readers to reevaluate their spending priorities, cut unnecessary fees, and strategically allocate resources to build a cash buffer.

A key topic explored is the importance of the emergence of finance. Readers are encouraged to proactively build and maintain a strong emergency fund that offers financial security at times of economic uncertainty. The chapter outlines strategies for creating and preserving emerge price spreads, ensing that individuals have a cash cushion to fall back on in times of need.

The chapter delves into debt management strategies customere economical downdowns. Provides insights into prioritizing debt repayment, negotiating favorable terms with creditors and exploring refinancing options. By strategically addressing debt, individuals can ease economic burdens and position their themselves for greater balance during a challenging economic climate.

Furthermore, "Navigating Economic Downturns" advocates a proactive approach to income diversification. Readers are encouraged to explore other sources of income, whether through side hustles, opportunities or investments. Diversification is not the handiest enhances of currency resilience, however it also paves the way for continued boom even in the face of economic challenges.

A fundamental aspect of this chapter is the exploration of mental resilience. Economic downturns can take a toll on mental well-being, and the chapter offers insights into maintaining a positive mindset, managing stress and seeking help. By promoting mental resilience, individuals can navigate challenges with a clear and focused mind and make informed decisions in the midst of uncertainty.

In essence, "Navigating Economic Downturns" is a comprehensive guide that equips readers with the equipment and mindset necessary to meet economic challenges head-on. By adopting proactive financial strategies, building resilience and maintaining a strategic outlook, individuals can not only weather economic downturns, but also emerge from them with a strong economic foundation and a lack of personal financial shortfalls.

Strategies for financial resilience during tough times

In the face of economic uncertainties and challenging circumstances, cultivating financial resilience becomes paramount. This chapter explores strategic approaches and practical measures to fortify one's financial position, enabling individuals to not only withstand tough times but also emerge stronger and more secure.

The chapter begins by emphasizing the importance of proactive financial planning. Readers are encouraged to assess their current financial situation, identify potential vulnerabilities, and create a comprehensive budget that aligns with their financial goals. This strategic planning serves as the foundation for building resilience and navigating tough times with a clear roadmap.

A central theme revolves around the creation and maintenance of emergency funds. The chapter provides actionable insights into establishing a robust financial safety net, emphasizing the need to set aside a dedicated fund to cover essential expenses during periods of financial hardship. Practical tips for consistently contributing to and preserving emergency funds are outlined, ensuring individuals have a buffer to rely on in times of need.

Debt management strategies take center stage as the chapter addresses the impact of tough economic conditions on personal finances. Readers are guided through prioritizing debt repayment, negotiating with creditors for favorable terms, and exploring options for restructuring or refinancing debt. By strategically managing debt, individuals can alleviate financial burdens and position themselves for greater resilience.

Income diversification emerges as a key strategy for weathering tough times. The chapter explores avenues for supplementing income, whether through side hustles, freelancing, or exploring alternative sources of revenue. Diversifying income streams not only provides a financial cushion but also enhances overall financial stability during challenging periods.

The chapter delves into the importance of revisiting and adjusting financial goals during tough times. It advocates for a realistic assessment of short-term and long-term objectives, acknowledging that flexibility and adaptability are crucial in the face of economic uncertainties. By recalibrating financial goals, individuals can align their aspirations with the current economic landscape and make informed decisions accordingly.

Psychological resilience is given due consideration in the chapter. Tough times can take a toll on mental well-being, and the chapter offers insights into maintaining a positive mindset, managing stress, and seeking support when needed. Cultivating psychological resilience is integral to making sound financial decisions and navigating tough times with a resilient outlook.

In summary, "Strategies for Financial Resilience During Tough Times" provides readers with a comprehensive toolkit for building and maintaining financial resilience. By proactively planning, creating emergency funds, strategically managing debt, diversifying income, and fostering psychological resilience, individuals can navigate challenging economic climates with confidence and emerge with a strengthened financial foundation.

Turning challenges into opportunities

In the complex dance of existence, challenging situations often appear as unexpected partners in the adventure of personal and financial growth. This bankruptcy explores the transformative mindset of turning challenges into possibility—a shift in angle that enables people not only to triumph over adversity, but in addition to use it as a catalyst for excellent alternative and development.

Bankruptcy begins by acknowledging the inevitability of challenges and emphasizing that they are a necessary part of the human pastime. Rather than viewing challenging situations as insurmountable constraints, we encourage readers to view them as stepping stones to non-public and economic improvement.

Central to this transformative thinking is the concept of resilience. Readers are guided to embrace resilience as a dynamic force that enables them to recover from setbacks, learn from adversity, and adapt to changing opportunities. By embracing resilience, individuals can handle challenges with a sense of electricity and strength.

A key subject of inquiry is the reframing of adversity as an opportunity for growth. This chapter delves into the concept that challenging situations often yield valuable lessons and insights. By approaching difficulties with curiosity and a willingness to explore, individuals can gain understanding from adversity, especially private and economic development.

In addition, the audition promotes a proactive attitude in the face of challenging situations. Instead of succumbing to a victim mentality, individuals are encouraged to take control of their response to adversity. This can include setting achievable dreams, breaking down challenging situations into manageable steps, and using support systems to tackle difficult opportunities.

The transformative way of thinking of turning challenging situations into opportunities also extends to the area of creating monetary withdrawals. Readers are guided to view monetary setbacks not as obstacles, but as opportunities to reassess and improve their monetary strategies. Additionally, this may include rethinking budgeting procedures, exploring new revenue streams, or strategically addressing debt in the face of economic challenges.

A key factor in this shift in thinking is the reframing of disasters as stepping stones to success. This chapter deals with the concept that setbacks and setbacks are not giving up, but alternative valuable messages that contribute to private and economic growth. By viewing failure as an opportunity to learn, adapt, and innovate, people can transform setbacks into stepping stones to destined success.

In essence, "Turning Challenges to Opportunities" is a rousing title that embraces a mindset that no longer sees adversity as an obstacle, but as a gateway to boom. By cultivating resilience, learning from challenges, taking proactive steps, and turning setbacks into opportunities, individuals can navigate life's complexities with a sense of empowerment and emerge from challenging situations with newfound electricity, information, and the potential to turn adversity into an effective force for subtle transformation.

9.2 Dealing with Unexpected Expenses

Life is inherently unpredictable and unforeseen eexpenses can crop up at the most unexpected moments, challenging our monetary stability. This chapter provides a strategic guide on how to navigate and effectively deal with unexpected expenses and ensure that people can manage financial surprises with resilience and practicality.

The chapter begins by acknowledging the inevitability of unexpected expenses, emphasizing that financial preparedness is a key part of a robust financial strategy. Readers are encouraged to cultivate a proactive mindset, recognizing that while the timing and nature of unexpected expenses may also be uncertain, their impact can be mitigated by strategic planning.

A central theme revolves around the importance of building and maintaining an emergency budget. The chapter provides realistic insights into the establishment of a dedicateded fund ecifically designed to cover uneexpected eexpenses. It guides readers on how to determine the appropriate size of an emergency fund based on personal circumstances and offers a monetary cushion to absorb the impact of unforeseen economic challenges.

This chapter further explores the importance of budgeting as a tool for dealing with unexpected expenses. Readers are encouraged to create flexible budgets that allow for unforeseen situations and unexpected prices. By building a buffer into the budget, people can navigate economic surprises without noticeably disrupting their overall money plan.

This chapter looks at the psychological aspects of coping with unexpected expenses, emphasizing the importance of staying calm and focused. It provides insight into stress management strategies and emphasizes that maintaining emotional well-being is integral to making sound money decisions in all challenging times.

Practical suggestions for negotiating and reducing unexpected expenses are given in the chapter. Whether negotiating medical payments, finding discounts, or researching payment plans, readers are guided on how to take proactive steps to ease the economic burden of unexpected costs.

Furthermore, this chapter advocates a proactive insurance coverage technique. It explores the importance of getting adequate insurance policies that include health insurance, home insurance and auto insurance to provide monetary protection in the event of unexpected events.

A key aspect of dealing with unexpected expenses is the ability to reassess and adjust your money dreams in response to the circumstances of the transfer. The chapter encourages the reader to be flexible in their economic planning plans, recognition that adapting to unexpected eexpenses may additionally involve a temporary change of priorities to adress immediate ne.

In essence, "Dealing with Unexpected Expenses" is a comprehensive guide that enables people to navigate monetary surprises with practicality and resilience. By cultivating a proactive mindset, constructing an emergency price range, incorporating flexibility into budgets, and preserving emotional well-being, people can effectively manage unexpected expenses and ensure that financial setbacks do no longer derail their overall economic well-being.

Creating contingency plans for unexpected financial burdens

In the dynamic landscape of personal finance, the ability to anticipate and navigate unexpected financial burdens is a hallmark of financial preparedness. This chapter provides a strategic blueprint for readers to create effective contingency plans, ensuring they are equipped to handle unforeseen challenges with resilience and foresight.

The chapter initiates by underlining the significance of proactive financial planning. Readers are prompted to adopt a forward-thinking mindset, recognizing that while it may be impossible to predict every financial curveball, having a well-thought-out contingency plan serves as a buffer against the uncertainties that life may present.

A central tenet revolves around the creation and maintenance of emergency funds. The chapter offers practical guidance on establishing a dedicated fund designed to absorb unexpected financial blows. Readers are led through the process of determining the optimal size of their emergency fund, taking into account factors such as monthly expenses, income variability, and the nature of potential financial shocks.

Moreover, the chapter explores the art of budgeting as a tool for crafting effective contingency plans. Readers are encouraged to develop flexible budgets that accommodate unexpected expenses. By incorporating a contingency line item, individuals can better navigate financial surprises without derailing their broader financial goals.

The chapter delves into the psychological aspect of preparing for unexpected financial burdens, emphasizing the importance of maintaining a calm and composed mindset. It provides insights into stress management strategies, highlighting that emotional well-being is pivotal when making sound financial decisions in the face of unforeseen challenges.

Practical tips for negotiating and mitigating unexpected expenses are outlined. Whether it involves negotiating medical bills, exploring payment plans, or seeking discounts, readers are empowered to take proactive measures to alleviate the financial impact of unexpected costs.

Furthermore, the chapter advocates for a proactive approach to insurance coverage. It explores the importance of having comprehensive insurance policies, such as health, home, and car insurance, to provide an additional layer of financial protection against unexpected events.

A key aspect of creating contingency plans is the ability to reassess and adjust financial goals in response to changing circumstances. The chapter encourages readers to cultivate adaptability, recognizing that addressing unexpected financial burdens may involve temporarily reprioritizing financial objectives to address immediate needs.

In essence, "Creating Contingency Plans for Unexpected Financial Burdens" is a comprehensive guide that empowers individuals to navigate the uncertainties of life with foresight and resilience. By cultivating a proactive mindset, building emergency funds, integrating flexibility into budgets, and prioritizing emotional well-being, individuals can construct robust contingency plans that enable them to weather unexpected financial storms and maintain their overall financial well-being.

Building a mindset of adaptability and resourcefulness

In the ever-evolving landscape of life, fostering a mindset of adaptability and resourcefulness is a transformative approach that empowers individuals to navigate challenges, seize opportunities, and thrive in the face of uncertainty. This chapter explores the key principles and practical strategies for cultivating a mindset that embraces change, leverages resources creatively, and turns obstacles into stepping stones for personal and financial growth.

The chapter begins by highlighting the dynamic nature of the world and the inevitability of change. Readers are encouraged to shift their perspective from viewing change as a disruption to embracing it as a constant force that presents possibilities for growth. Acknowledging that life is inherently unpredictable lays the foundation for developing a resilient and adaptive mindset.

A central theme revolves around adaptability—a willingness to adjust, learn, and evolve in response to changing circumstances. The chapter guides readers to embrace change as an opportunity for personal development. It encourages them to proactively seek new skills, stay informed about emerging trends, and view challenges as avenues for acquiring valuable experiences that contribute to personal and financial growth.

Resourcefulness takes center stage as the chapter explores creative problem-solving and making the most of available resources. Readers are prompted to view limitations not as roadblocks but as catalysts for innovation. Strategies for maximizing efficiency, repurposing resources, and finding alternative solutions are presented, empowering individuals to navigate constraints with ingenuity.

Moreover, the chapter delves into the psychology of resilience. Building a resilient mindset involves developing emotional fortitude, maintaining optimism in the face of setbacks, and bouncing back from challenges with renewed determination. Readers are guided on how to cultivate mental resilience, turning adversity into an opportunity for strengthening their psychological well-being.

Practical tips for building a mindset of adaptability and resourcefulness are outlined throughout the chapter. From fostering a curiosity for learning and seeking diverse perspectives to embracing change as a constant in life, individuals are empowered to proactively shape their mindset for success in a rapidly changing world.

The transformative power of adaptability and resourcefulness is further explored in the context of personal finance. Readers are encouraged to apply these principles to financial decision-making, such as navigating market fluctuations, adjusting investment strategies, and creatively addressing financial challenges.

In essence, "Building a Mindset of Adaptability and Resourcefulness" serves as a guide for readers to cultivate a mindset that not only embraces change but leverages it as a catalyst for personal and financial advancement. By fostering adaptability, resourcefulness, and resilience, individuals can navigate the complexities of life with confidence, turning challenges into opportunities for growth and transformation.

Chapter 10:

Behavioral Economics and Money Mastery

In a complex dance between psychology and finance, Chapter 10 delves into the fascinating realm of behavioral economics and its profound implications for mastering the art of money. This chapter serves as a guide for readers to understand the complexities of human behavior in economic decision-making, providing insights that enable them to navigate the economic landscape with expertise and foresight.

The chapter begins with the help of uncovering the basic principles of behavioral economics. Readers are introduced to the belief that human decision-making is now influenced not only by rational considerations, but also by cognitive biases, emotions, and social factors. Understanding these behavioral nuances lays the foundation for a deeper exploration of how individuals can use this knowledge for financial mastery.

The central theme revolves around the concept of cognitive biases and their influence on financial choices. This chapter sheds light on common biases, including loss aversion, overconfidence, and the anchoring effect, illustrating how these biases can lead people astray when making monetary decisions. By recognizing these cognitive pitfalls, readers can develop a heightened awareness that serves as a shield against impulsive or irrational financial choices.

This chapter further explores the role of emotions in economic decision-making. He delves into the psychology of money and reveals how emotions like fear, greed and euphoria can influence economic choices. Readers are guided on how to cultivate emotional intelligence, make informed decisions that align with their long-term financial goals, while navigating the emotional currents that often accompany financial matters.

Practical behavioral economics programs are woven into the fabric of money mastery. This chapter provides actionable strategies for using behavioral insights to improve financial discipline, cultivate healthy spending, and build a resilient mindset that withstands the challenges of the money market.

The concept of nudges and choice architecture is explored as a device for guiding monetary decisions in a positive direction. By understanding how the presentation of options can influence decision making, readers are empowered to design their financial environment in ways that support their dreams and minimize behavioral impact.

Furthermore, this chapter examines the social aspects of economic behavior. It sheds mild on the influence of social norms, peer pressure, and societal eexpectations on monetary choices. Readers are encouraged to consciously navigate social influences and align their money decisions with their values and long-term aspirations.

In essence, "Behavioral Economics and Money Mastery" uncovers the hidden forces shaping financial decisions and equips readers with the knowledge to manage these influences. By combining the principles of behavioral economics with sound strategies, people can create a path to monetary mastery that is informed, resilient, and aligned with their unique economic dreams and aspirations.

10.1 The Psychology of Financial Decision-Making

Chapter 10 delves into the intricate interplay between the human mind and financial choices, unraveling the psychology that underlies the decisions individuals make in managing their money. This chapter serves as a comprehensive exploration of the cognitive and emotional factors influencing financial decision-making, empowering readers with insights to make informed and mindful choices on their financial journey.

The chapter commences by delving into the cognitive dimensions of decision-making. Readers are introduced to the rational and analytical aspects that govern financial choices. Concepts such as risk assessment, cost-benefit analysis, and the influence of past experiences are explored, providing a foundational understanding of how cognitive processes shape financial decisions.

A central theme revolves around the impact of emotions on financial choices. The chapter elucidates the role of emotions such as fear, greed, and excitement in influencing financial behaviors. By recognizing the emotional underpinnings of decision-making, readers gain a deeper awareness of how feelings can either align with or diverge from rational financial goals.

Cognitive biases take center stage as the chapter unveils the common mental shortcuts and patterns that can lead to suboptimal financial decisions. Concepts like confirmation bias, availability heuristic, and anchoring are demystified, enabling readers to identify and mitigate the influence of these biases in their financial choices.

Moreover, the chapter explores the concept of temporal discounting—the tendency to prioritize immediate rewards over future gains. Readers are guided on how to navigate this temporal bias, fostering a mindset that values long-term financial objectives over short-term gratification.

Practical applications of psychological insights are woven into the fabric of financial decision-making. Readers are equipped with strategies to mitigate the impact of cognitive biases and emotional influences, fostering a balanced approach that aligns with their overarching financial goals.

The chapter also highlights the importance of financial self-awareness. Readers are encouraged to engage in reflective practices, understanding their own risk tolerance, money attitudes, and the psychological factors that may influence their financial choices. This self-awareness serves as a cornerstone for making decisions that resonate with individual values and aspirations.

In essence, "The Psychology of Financial Decision-Making" unravels the complex web of cognitive and emotional factors that shape how individuals manage their finances. By comprehending the interplay between rational thought, emotions, and cognitive biases, readers gain a nuanced understanding of their own decision-making processes. Armed with this awareness, they can navigate the psychological landscape of finance with mindfulness, making choices that align with their long-term financial well-being.

Understanding behavioral economics principles

Behavioral economics, at its core, explores the fascinating intersection of psychology and economics, revealing how human behavior deviates from the traditional assumptions of rational decision-making in economic theory. This chapter serves as a comprehensive guide to understanding the key principles that define behavioral economics, shedding light on the cognitive biases, emotional influences, and social factors that shape the choices individuals make in the realm of finance.

The chapter commences by unraveling the foundational concept of bounded rationality. Unlike classical economic theories that assume individuals make decisions with perfect rationality, behavioral economics recognizes that human cognitive resources are limited. Readers are introduced to the idea that decision-makers often rely on heuristics—mental shortcuts—to navigate the complexities of decision-making efficiently.

A central theme revolves around the concept of cognitive biases. The chapter demystifies common biases such as confirmation bias, anchoring, and overconfidence, illustrating how these mental shortcuts can lead individuals to deviate from rational decision-making. By understanding these biases, readers gain insights into the quirks and pitfalls of the human mind that impact financial choices.

Moreover, the chapter explores the psychological phenomenon of loss aversion. Readers are guided to comprehend how the fear of losses often outweighs the desire for gains, influencing decision-makers to take risks or avoid losses in ways that may not align with traditional economic predictions. This principle lies at the heart of understanding why individuals may act irrationally in certain financial situations.

The social aspects of decision-making are also illuminated in the chapter. Readers discover how social norms, peer influence, and the desire for social approval play a pivotal role in shaping financial behaviors. Behavioral economics recognizes that individuals don't make decisions in isolation but are influenced by the social contexts in which they operate.

Practical applications of behavioral economics principles are interwoven throughout the chapter. Readers are equipped with insights into how these principles manifest in everyday financial decisions, from investment choices to spending patterns. By grasping these principles, individuals can make more informed decisions and navigate the complexities of financial choices with a nuanced understanding of their own behavioral tendencies.

In essence, "Understanding Behavioral Economics Principles" serves as a compass for readers navigating the intricate terrain where psychology meets economics. By comprehending the limitations of human cognition, recognizing cognitive biases, and understanding the social influences on decision-making, individuals can approach financial choices with a heightened awareness that aligns with the realities of human behavior.

Applying psychology to enhance financial decision-making

Chapter 10 is a practical exploration into the application of psychological principles to elevate financial decision-making. Readers embark on a journey that goes beyond understanding the intricacies of human behavior in finance; this chapter empowers them to leverage psychological insights effectively, making informed and strategic choices on their financial path.

The chapter begins by emphasizing the actionable nature of psychological principles. Readers are prompted to see psychology not merely as an abstract concept but as a toolkit for improving financial decision-making. By acknowledging the role of emotions, cognitive biases, and social factors, individuals can harness these insights to navigate the financial landscape more effectively.

A central theme revolves around emotional intelligence and its impact on financial choices. The chapter guides readers in recognizing and managing their emotions in financial decision-making. Strategies for cultivating emotional resilience, making decisions under stress, and staying focused on long-term goals despite emotional fluctuations are explored.

Moreover, the chapter delves into the practical application of cognitive biases. Readers are equipped with tools to identify and mitigate biases in their decision-making process. By understanding how biases such as loss aversion and overconfidence can sway choices, individuals can implement strategies to counteract their impact and make more rational financial decisions.

The social dimension of financial decisions is also explored. Readers discover how to navigate social pressures, peer influences, and societal expectations. By applying psychological insights to understand their own motivations in a social context, individuals can align their financial choices with personal values rather than succumbing to external pressures.

Practical exercises and real-life scenarios are integrated throughout the chapter. Readers engage in reflective practices to assess their own emotional responses, identify cognitive biases in past decisions, and evaluate the social influences on their financial choices. These exercises serve as a hands-on approach to applying psychological principles in a personalized and meaningful way.

The chapter concludes with a call to action, encouraging readers to actively incorporate psychological strategies into their financial decision-making toolkit. By viewing psychology not as a passive observer but as an active participant in the decision-making process, individuals can enhance their financial acumen and make choices that resonate with their values and long-term objectives.

In essence, "Applying Psychology to Enhance Financial Decision-Making" transforms psychological insights into actionable tools. By weaving emotional intelligence, cognitive awareness, and social understanding into financial choices, readers can navigate the complexities of finance with a heightened level of self-awareness, resilience, and strategic decision-making.

10.2 Cognitive Biases and Money Management

This part delves into the captivating realm where cognitive biases intersect with money management. As we navigate the intricate landscape of personal finance, understanding and mitigating these biases becomes paramount. This chapter serves as a comprehensive guide, unraveling the impact of cognitive biases on financial decisions and equipping readers with strategies to navigate these biases effectively.

The chapter initiates by demystifying the concept of cognitive biases. These biases, rooted in mental shortcuts and patterns of thinking, can significantly influence decision-making. Readers are introduced to the notion that, despite our best intentions, our minds often deviate from rationality, impacting the way we manage our finances.

A central theme revolves around the confirmation bias—an inclination to favor information that aligns with pre-existing beliefs. The chapter explores how this bias can shape financial choices, influencing everything from investment decisions to spending patterns. By recognizing and mitigating the confirmation bias, readers can cultivate a more objective and evidence-based approach to money management.

Moreover, the chapter delves into the anchoring bias—a tendency to rely too heavily on the first piece of information encountered. Readers discover how this bias can impact financial negotiations, budgeting, and investment decisions. Strategies for overcoming the anchoring bias are presented, empowering individuals to make more well-informed financial choices.

The availability heuristic takes center stage as the chapter explores how individuals often rely on readily available information rather than seeking out comprehensive data. This bias can lead to suboptimal financial decisions. By understanding the availability heuristic, readers are encouraged to seek a broader range of information, enhancing their decision-making process.

Practical applications of cognitive bias awareness are woven throughout the chapter. Readers engage in exercises to identify and reflect on how biases may have influenced past financial decisions. By developing this heightened self-awareness, individuals can actively work to counteract the impact of biases in their money management practices.

The chapter concludes by emphasizing the ongoing nature of cognitive bias management in money matters. Readers are encouraged to integrate these insights into their financial toolkit, creating a proactive approach to decision-making that recognizes and mitigates the influence of cognitive biases.

In essence, "Cognitive Biases and Money Management" is a roadmap for readers to navigate the intricate relationship between the quirks of the mind and financial choices. By understanding, identifying, and actively managing cognitive biases, individuals can enhance their money management skills, making decisions that align more closely with their long-term financial goals.

Identifying and overcoming common cognitive biases

This part serves as a practical guide to help readers navigate the often-hidden terrain of cognitive biases that influence decision-making. Recognizing the pervasive impact of these biases on our financial choices, this chapter offers insights and strategies to identify and overcome common cognitive biases, empowering individuals to make more rational and informed decisions.

The chapter begins by demystifying the concept of cognitive biases, emphasizing their prevalence in decision-making. Readers are guided to understand that these biases are systematic errors in thinking that can lead us astray from rationality, particularly in the realm of money management.

A central theme revolves around the confirmation bias—the tendency to seek, interpret, and favor information that confirms pre-existing beliefs. Readers are prompted to reflect on how this bias might have influenced past financial decisions and are equipped with strategies to overcome it. By actively seeking diverse perspectives and challenging existing beliefs, individuals can mitigate the impact of the confirmation bias.

Moreover, the chapter delves into the anchoring bias—a reliance on the first piece of information encountered when making decisions. Practical tips are provided to help readers recognize instances where anchoring may occur in financial contexts, such as negotiations or budgeting. By consciously re-evaluating information and avoiding undue influence from initial data, individuals can make more objective financial decisions.

The availability heuristic takes center stage as the chapter explores how individuals often base decisions on readily available information rather than a comprehensive assessment of facts. Readers are encouraged to broaden their information sources and critically evaluate the reliability of data to counteract the influence of the availability heuristic in financial decision-making.

Practical applications are interwoven throughout the chapter, guiding readers through exercises to identify and reflect on how these biases may have impacted their financial choices. By developing a heightened self-awareness, individuals can actively work towards recognizing and overcoming cognitive biases in their money management practices.

The chapter concludes with a call to action, encouraging readers to integrate these strategies into their ongoing decision-making processes. By fostering a mindset of curiosity, embracing diverse viewpoints, and maintaining vigilance against cognitive biases, individuals can enhance their ability to make sound and objective financial decisions.

In essence, "Identifying and Overcoming Common Cognitive Biases" serves as a roadmap for readers to navigate the intricate landscape of decision-making. By understanding, identifying, and actively mitigating cognitive biases, individuals empower themselves to make financial choices that align more closely with their long-term goals and objectives.

Making informed and rational financial choices

Within the landscape of personal finance, the ability to make informed and rational decisions is a cornerstone of financial well-being. In this section, we delve into practical strategies to cultivate a mindset that aligns with rational decision-making, promoting financial success and stability.

The chapter begins by emphasizing the significance of making choices founded on reliable information and objective analysis. In a world filled with financial complexities, the pursuit of knowledge and the commitment to rationality become invaluable tools in navigating various money-related decisions.

A central theme revolves around the importance of thorough research and due diligence. Readers are encouraged to seek out diverse sources of information, critically evaluate data, and consider multiple perspectives before arriving at financial decisions. This approach mitigates the impact of cognitive biases and ensures that choices are grounded in a well-rounded understanding of the situation.

Moreover, the chapter explores the concept of goal-oriented decision-making. By defining clear financial goals, individuals can align their choices with their overarching objectives. Whether it's saving for a home, investing for retirement, or paying off debt, having a well-defined set of goals provides a compass for rational decision-making in the face of various financial options.

Practical applications are woven into the fabric of the chapter, guiding readers on how to implement these strategies in their daily financial choices. Exercises prompt reflection on personal financial goals, sources of information, and decision-making processes, fostering a proactive and intentional approach to money management.

The chapter concludes by reinforcing the idea that making informed and rational financial choices is an ongoing journey. It requires continuous learning, self-reflection, and adaptation to changing circumstances. By embracing a mindset that values rationality, individuals equip themselves with the tools needed to navigate the dynamic landscape of personal finance successfully.

In essence, "Making Informed and Rational Financial Choices" serves as a beacon for readers, guiding them towards a path where decisions are grounded in knowledge, free from the influence of cognitive biases, and aligned with their unique financial aspirations.

Chapter 11:

Sustainable Wealth and Giving Back

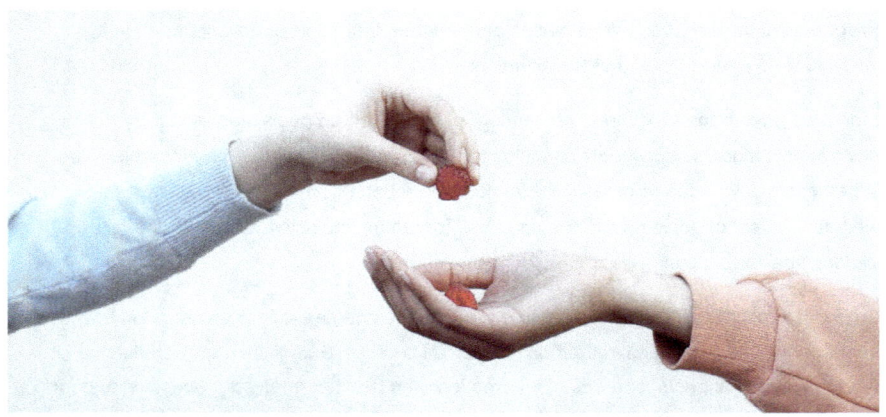

In this pivotal chapter, we explore the profound intersection of financial success and social responsibility. "Sustainable Wealth and Giving Back" transcends traditional notions of prosperity by delving into the transformative power of using wealth as a force for positive change.

The chapter begins by redefining wealth, emphasizing that true affluence extends beyond monetary value. Readers are invited to envision wealth as a holistic concept that encompasses financial well-being, societal impact, and a sense of fulfillment. The narrative unfolds to showcase how sustainable wealth involves not only the accumulation of assets but also their purposeful utilization for the betterment of oneself and society.

A central theme revolves around the concept of giving back. Readers are encouraged to explore philanthropy as a means to leverage their financial success for the greater good. Whether through charitable donations, community initiatives, or sustainable investments, the chapter elucidates how giving back can create a positive ripple effect, contributing to the well-being of communities and the world at large.

Moreover, the chapter explores the principles of sustainable wealth management. It guides readers on crafting a financial legacy that endures for future generations, emphasizing responsible investment choices and environmentally conscious financial practices. The narrative unfolds to showcase that sustainable wealth is not only about the present but also about leaving a positive impact for the future.

Practical applications are woven throughout the chapter, offering readers tangible strategies for incorporating sustainable wealth practices into their financial journey. From ethical investing to conscious consumerism, readers are empowered to make choices that align with both their financial goals and their commitment to creating a positive societal impact.

The chapter concludes by underscoring the idea that sustainable wealth and giving back are not only attainable but also essential components of a truly fulfilling financial journey. By embracing a mindset that integrates financial success with social responsibility, individuals embark on a path towards creating a legacy that extends beyond personal prosperity, leaving a lasting positive imprint on the world.

In essence, "Chapter 11: Sustainable Wealth and Giving Back" invites readers to envision wealth through a broader lens—one that encompasses not only financial prosperity but also the profound impact one can make in fostering a better, more sustainable world.

11.1 Achieving Sustainable Wealth

In the pursuit of financial success, "Achieving Sustainable Wealth" challenges the conventional view of wealth as merely a monetary measure. This section invites readers to explore a more holistic perspective, where wealth encompasses not only financial stability but also a commitment to social responsibility and a lasting legacy.

We start by redefining wealth, emphasizing its sustainability and broader impact. Here, wealth is not seen solely as the accumulation of assets but as a dynamic force capable of contributing positively to personal fulfillment and societal well-being.

A central theme revolves around responsible wealth management. This involves making conscious and ethical financial decisions, from investments aligned with social and environmental values to adopting sustainable spending practices. The goal is to integrate sustainability seamlessly into one's wealth-building strategies.

Moreover, we explore the concept of financial stewardship. Readers are encouraged to view their wealth not just as a measure of individual success but as a tool for creating positive and lasting impacts. Sustainable wealth is portrayed as an ongoing journey, requiring mindful decision-making and a commitment to leaving a legacy that extends beyond immediate financial gains.

Practical applications are interwoven throughout, offering readers actionable steps to make sustainable choices in their financial journey. Whether through responsible investing, philanthropy, or adopting eco-friendly financial practices, individuals are empowered to align their wealth-building efforts with values that prioritize long-term well-being.

In conclusion, "Achieving Sustainable Wealth" is an exploration into a more meaningful and fulfilling approach to financial success. By embracing a perspective that integrates financial wisdom, ethical considerations, and a commitment to societal well-being, readers can navigate their financial journey with purpose and contribute to a sustainable and prosperous future.

Long-term strategies for maintaining financial freedom

In the pursuit of sustained financial freedom, it is crucial to adopt long-term strategies that ensure stability and resilience. This section explores practical and enduring approaches to maintain financial freedom over the course of a lifetime.

Diversified Investments: Building and maintaining a diverse investment portfolio is key to long-term financial freedom. Spread investments across different asset classes to mitigate risks and capitalize on opportunities, fostering a resilient financial foundation.

Continuous Learning and Adaptation: The financial landscape evolves, and so should your financial knowledge. Commit to continuous learning about personal finance, investment strategies, and economic trends. This adaptability ensures that you can make informed decisions in changing circumstances.

Emergency Fund Reinforcement: Regularly assess and reinforce your emergency fund. Having a robust financial safety net protects you from unexpected expenses and provides peace of mind during economic uncertainties.

Debt Management: Strive to minimize and responsibly manage debt. Implement effective debt reduction strategies, and avoid accumulating high-interest debts. This not only ensures financial stability but also frees up resources for wealth-building.

Smart Lifestyle Choices: Make conscious and sustainable lifestyle choices that align with your financial goals. Avoid excessive spending on non-essential items and focus on experiences and investments that contribute to your long-term well-being.

Regular Financial Check-ups: Schedule periodic reviews of your financial plan. Assess your progress, adjust goals if necessary, and ensure that your financial strategies are aligned with your evolving life circumstances.

Insurance Protection: Invest in comprehensive insurance coverage to safeguard against unforeseen events. Adequate health, life, and property insurance provide a safety net that protects your financial freedom in times of crisis.

Strategic Retirement Planning: Plan for a secure retirement by consistently contributing to retirement accounts. Utilize tax-advantaged retirement plans and consider diversifying retirement investments to ensure a stable income stream in your later years.

Income Diversification: Explore opportunities to diversify your income streams. This might include side businesses, investments, or passive income sources, providing resilience against economic fluctuations and job uncertainties.

Estate Planning: Develop a comprehensive estate plan to secure the financial well-being of future generations. This includes creating wills, trusts, and specifying your wishes for the distribution of assets.

Regular Budget Assessments: Periodically review and adjust your budget to reflect changing financial goals and circumstances. This ensures that your spending aligns with your priorities and that you are consistently working towards financial freedom.

By incorporating these long-term strategies into your financial approach, you not only achieve financial freedom but also sustain it over time. These principles emphasize adaptability, strategic planning, and a holistic approach to financial well-being.

Balancing personal and financial well-being

Achieving a harmonious balance between personal fulfillment and financial stability is a nuanced journey that requires intentional choices and mindful practices. This section explores key principles to help individuals strike a meaningful equilibrium between personal well-being and financial success.

Define Personal Values and Goals: Begin by clearly defining your personal values and life goals. Understanding what truly matters to you provides a foundation for aligning your financial decisions with your broader aspirations.

Create a Holistic Financial Plan: Develop a financial plan that not only focuses on monetary objectives but also incorporates personal goals and lifestyle preferences. This comprehensive approach ensures that your financial decisions support your overall well-being.

Practice Mindful Spending: Cultivate mindfulness in your spending habits. Prioritize expenditures that align with your values and contribute to your happiness. Mindful spending involves making intentional choices that bring joy and satisfaction, rather than impulsive or emotional purchases.

Establish Healthy Financial Habits: Incorporate positive financial habits into your routine. This includes budgeting, saving, and investing responsibly. These habits not only contribute to financial well-being but also alleviate stress associated with money management.

Work-Life Balance: Recognize the importance of a healthy work-life balance. While career success is vital, it should not come at the expense of your well-being. Set boundaries, prioritize self-care, and allocate time for personal pursuits to foster a balanced lifestyle.

Embrace Minimalism: Consider adopting minimalist principles in your lifestyle. Simplifying possessions and focusing on experiences over material goods can contribute to both personal and financial well-being.

Invest in Personal Development: Allocate resources for personal growth and development. This could include education, hobbies, or activities that enhance your well-being. Investing in yourself contributes to a more fulfilling life.

Regularly Reassess Priorities: Life is dynamic, and priorities evolve. Regularly reassess your personal and financial goals to ensure they remain aligned with your current circumstances and aspirations.

Prioritize Mental and Physical Health: Recognize the intrinsic connection between physical and financial well-being. Prioritize activities that promote mental and physical health, understanding that a healthy lifestyle contributes to a more robust financial future.

Build a Supportive Network: Surround yourself with a supportive network of friends and family. Social connections play a significant role in overall well-being, providing emotional support during both personal and financial challenges.

Celebrate Achievements: Acknowledge and celebrate milestones, both personal and financial. Recognizing achievements, no matter how small, fosters a positive mindset and reinforces the connection between personal fulfillment and financial success.

In essence, balancing personal and financial well-being is an ongoing and intentional process. By aligning your financial decisions with your values, nurturing personal growth, and fostering a healthy lifestyle, you can create a life that is not only financially sound but also deeply fulfilling.

11.2 The Power of Giving Back

In the tapestry of personal and societal fulfillment, the act of giving back emerges as a transformative force. This section explores the profound impact of philanthropy and community engagement, shedding light on the enriching journey that unfolds when individuals embrace the power of giving.

Fostering a Sense of Purpose: Giving back instills a profound sense of purpose and meaning. Whether through charitable donations, volunteering, or community initiatives, the act of contributing to the well-being of others connects individuals to a larger purpose beyond personal achievements.

Creating Positive Social Impact: Philanthropy serves as a catalyst for positive social change. By supporting causes aligned with one's values, individuals contribute to addressing societal challenges, fostering inclusivity, and building a better world for current and future generations.

Building Empathy and Compassion: Engaging in acts of generosity cultivates empathy and compassion. Understanding the needs of others and actively working to alleviate suffering nurtures a sense of interconnectedness and solidarity with the broader human experience.

Enhancing Personal Fulfillment: The act of giving is inherently rewarding. Beyond the tangible impact on communities, individuals experience a deep sense of fulfillment and satisfaction when they witness the positive outcomes of their contributions.

Strengthening Community Bonds: Giving back creates a sense of community and strengthens social bonds. Collaborating with others who share similar values and goals amplifies the collective impact, fostering a spirit of unity and cooperation.

Inspiring Positive Change: Philanthropy serves as a beacon of inspiration. By leading through example, individuals inspire others to join the movement of giving, creating a ripple effect that amplifies the potential for positive change on a broader scale.

Promoting Personal Growth: The journey of giving back is a catalyst for personal growth. It challenges individuals to step outside their comfort zones, develop leadership skills, and gain a broader perspective on the world and its diverse challenges.

Cultivating Gratitude: The act of giving invites reflection on one's own blessings and privileges. Gratitude emerges as a natural companion to philanthropy, fostering a heightened appreciation for the positive aspects of one's own life.

Leaving a Lasting Legacy: Through philanthropic endeavors, individuals contribute to building a lasting legacy. The impact of their generosity extends beyond their lifetime, creating a positive imprint on the world and inspiring future generations.

Connecting with Community Values: Aligning giving efforts with community values creates a shared sense of responsibility and stewardship. This alignment ensures that philanthropic endeavors resonate with the unique needs and aspirations of the communities being served.

In summary, "The Power of Giving Back" transcends a mere act; it embodies a transformative force that elevates both the giver and the recipient. As individuals embrace the joy of contributing to the greater good, they become architects of positive change, weaving a narrative of compassion, purpose, and collective well-being.

Incorporating philanthropy into financial plans

Integrating philanthropy into financial plans is a powerful way to align personal values with financial goals, fostering a sense of purpose and contributing to positive societal impact. Here are strategic steps to seamlessly weave philanthropy into your financial journey:

Define Your Philanthropic Vision:

Begin by clarifying your philanthropic vision. What causes or issues align with your values? Identifying your passion areas establishes a foundation for meaningful giving.

Set Philanthropic Goals:

Establish clear and achievable philanthropic goals. Determine the scale of your giving, whether through regular donations, one-time contributions, or planned giving strategies.

Incorporate Philanthropy into Budgeting:

Allocate a specific portion of your budget to philanthropy. Treating charitable giving as a financial priority ensures consistency and allows you to plan for your contributions.

Research and Due Diligence:

Conduct thorough research on potential charitable organizations. Verify their credibility, mission alignment, and the impact of their initiatives. Informed giving maximizes the effectiveness of your contributions.

Explore Tax-Advantaged Giving:

Investigate tax-advantaged giving options. Contributions to eligible charitable organizations may qualify for tax deductions, providing financial benefits while supporting causes you care about.

Consider Donor-Advised Funds:

Donor-Advised Funds (DAFs) offer a strategic way to manage charitable giving. They allow you to contribute assets, receive immediate tax benefits, and recommend grants to charitable organizations over time.

Integrate Philanthropy into Financial Goals:

Align your philanthropic goals with broader financial objectives. Consider how your giving aligns with savings, investment, and retirement plans to ensure a holistic approach.

Explore Impact Investing:

Investigate impact investing opportunities. This involves making investments that generate both financial returns and positive social or environmental impact, providing a dual benefit to your financial and philanthropic goals.

Engage Family in the Process:

If applicable, involve your family in the philanthropic decision-making process. This fosters a shared sense of purpose and allows each family member to contribute to causes they are passionate about.

Regularly Review and Adjust:

Periodically review your philanthropic strategy. Assess the impact of your contributions, explore new causes, and adjust your giving plan to reflect changing personal and societal needs.

Seek Professional Guidance:

Consult with financial advisors who specialize in philanthropy. They can provide tailored guidance on optimizing your giving strategy, including tax implications and estate planning considerations.

Share Your Philanthropic Story:

Consider sharing your philanthropic journey. Whether through social media, community engagement, or workplace initiatives, sharing your story can inspire others and amplify the impact of your giving.

In essence, incorporating philanthropy into financial plans is a deliberate and rewarding process that goes beyond monetary transactions. By thoughtfully integrating giving into your financial journey, you contribute to positive change while deriving personal fulfillment from your impact on the causes that matter most to you.

Creating a positive impact on the community

The endeavor to create a positive impact on the community is a journey of purpose, compassion, and shared responsibility. It transcends individual achievements, weaving a narrative of collective well-being and interconnectedness. At its core, community impact is a commitment to fostering positive change in the lives of those around us and leaving a lasting legacy that echoes through generations.

Central to this mission is the cultivation of empathy—an understanding of the diverse challenges, aspirations, and narratives that characterize a community. It involves stepping into the shoes of others, acknowledging their struggles, and recognizing the inherent dignity and worth of every individual. Through this lens of empathy, the path to meaningful impact begins to unfold.

Philanthropy becomes a cornerstone in the pursuit of community betterment. It is not merely about financial contributions but a strategic and intentional investment in initiatives that address the specific needs and aspirations of the community. Whether supporting education, healthcare, environmental sustainability, or social justice, philanthropy becomes a vehicle for translating empathy into tangible solutions.

Beyond financial contributions, the power of community impact lies in active engagement and collaboration. It involves rolling up sleeves, volunteering time and skills, and becoming an integral part of the community fabric. From mentoring programs that uplift the younger generation to participation in local initiatives that enhance environmental sustainability, the commitment to creating positive change is realized through hands-on involvement.

Education emerges as a linchpin in the journey to community impact. Empowering individuals with knowledge and skills equips them to navigate challenges, seize opportunities, and contribute meaningfully to the community's growth. Educational initiatives, mentorship programs, and skill-building workshops become catalysts for positive transformation, laying the groundwork for a thriving and empowered community.

Sustainable development takes center stage in the pursuit of community impact. It entails thoughtful planning and initiatives that not only address immediate needs but also ensure the long-term well-being of the community. Environmental stewardship, economic empowerment, and social inclusivity become integral components, creating a holistic framework for sustained positive change.

The ripple effect of community impact extends far beyond the immediate vicinity. It inspires a sense of pride, unity, and shared purpose among community members. As positive changes accumulate, a self-perpetuating cycle of growth and empowerment takes hold. Individuals feel a heightened sense of belonging, and the community becomes a beacon of resilience, collaboration, and hope.

In conclusion, creating a positive impact on the community is not a singular act but an ongoing commitment to empathy, philanthropy, education, and sustainable development. It is a testament to the belief that, collectively, individuals have the power to shape a community that is not only thriving in the present but poised for a resilient and vibrant future. Through these intentional efforts, the narrative of community impact becomes a story of shared triumph, resilience, and the enduring capacity for positive change.

Chapter 12:

Celebrating Financial Milestones

In the tapestry of one's financial journey, "Celebrating Financial Milestones" stands as a chapter of reflection, gratitude, and acknowledgment. It marks not only the culmination of diligent efforts but also a pause to recognize the significance of progress made on the path to financial freedom.

This chapter invites a moment of introspection, encouraging individuals to revisit the goals they set, the challenges they overcame, and the lessons they learned. It emphasizes the importance of acknowledging the incremental victories, both big and small, that collectively contribute to the broader narrative of financial success.

The celebration of financial milestones extends beyond mere numbers. It is a recognition of discipline, resilience, and the commitment to a vision of a more secure and fulfilling future. Whether it's reaching a savings target, paying off debts, or achieving investment goals, each milestone becomes a testament to the dedication invested in building a solid financial foundation.

Moreover, this chapter underscores the role of celebration in reinforcing positive financial habits. It is a reminder that the journey to financial freedom is not solely about reaching a destination but about embracing a mindset and lifestyle that align with one's aspirations. The act of celebration becomes a catalyst for continued motivation and a source of inspiration for the chapters yet to unfold.

As individuals commemorate their financial milestones, they are prompted to set new goals and aspirations. This cyclical process of setting, achieving, and celebrating milestones propels the financial journey forward, ensuring that it remains dynamic, purposeful, and attuned to evolving life circumstances.

In essence, "Celebrating Financial Milestones" encapsulates more than just numerical achievements. It encapsulates a moment of reflection, a pause to express gratitude for the journey so far, and a springboard for envisioning an even more prosperous and fulfilling financial future. This chapter serves as a reminder that each step taken on the financial path is a cause for celebration—a marker of progress on the road to enduring financial well-being.

12.1 Tracking and Celebrating Progress

In the intricate dance of financial mastery, the chapter titled "Tracking and Celebrating Progress" emerges as a pivotal juncture, inviting individuals to engage in a reflective exploration of their financial journey. It is a narrative woven with threads of diligence, resilience, and the sheer tenacity required to navigate the complexities of personal finance.

The essence of this chapter lies in its dual purpose: tracking and celebrating. It encourages a systematic review of financial milestones, allowing individuals to assess the distance covered from the starting point of their financial goals. This reflective exercise serves as a compass, guiding them to acknowledge the strides made, lessons learned, and hurdles overcome.

The process of tracking progress becomes a mirror reflecting the financial landscape. It involves a meticulous examination of budgetary allocations, investment returns, debt reduction, and savings growth. The objective is not merely to scrutinize numbers but to gain a deeper understanding of the financial ecosystem—an understanding that empowers individuals to make informed decisions and course corrections where necessary.

Amidst the scrutiny of financial metrics, there lies an equally significant aspect: celebrating progress. This celebration is not confined to the achievement of monumental goals but extends to the recognition of incremental victories. Whether it's consistently adhering to a budget, resisting impulsive purchases, or consistently contributing to savings, these smaller triumphs collectively contribute to the tapestry of financial success.

Celebration is not a mere formality; it is a vital component in the cultivation of a positive financial mindset. It reinforces the discipline and habits that underpin financial well-being. By acknowledging and celebrating progress, individuals imbue their financial journey with a sense of accomplishment and motivation. This positive reinforcement becomes a self-perpetuating cycle, propelling them toward more ambitious goals with newfound vigor.

Moreover, this chapter serves as a dynamic tool for recalibration. It prompts individuals to revisit and adjust their financial goals in light of changing life circumstances, economic landscapes, and personal aspirations. The ability to adapt and refine goals ensures that the financial journey remains fluid, responsive, and aligned with evolving life narratives.

In essence, "Tracking and Celebrating Progress" is a chapter of introspection, revelation, and jubilation. It encapsulates the journey from financial inception to the present moment and becomes a compass for charting the course ahead. Through the lens of tracking and celebration, individuals not only measure their financial growth but infuse their journey with a spirit of positivity, resilience, and an unwavering commitment to unlocking the full spectrum of financial freedom.

Establishing milestones for financial success

In the grand tapestry of financial freedom, the chapter titled "Establishing Milestones for Financial Success" serves as the architectural blueprint—a strategic and intentional guide for individuals navigating the landscape of personal finance. It is within this chapter that the seeds of vision are sown, and the foundation for a secure and prosperous financial future is carefully laid.

At its essence, the establishment of financial milestones is a forward-looking endeavor, requiring individuals to envision their desired destination and delineate the incremental steps leading to it. These milestones are not arbitrary markers but purposeful goals that align with one's unique aspirations, values, and life circumstances.

The process commences with a thorough self-examination—a deep dive into one's financial landscape, aspirations, and potential roadblocks. It involves contemplating life goals, be they short-term or long-term, and understanding the financial commitments that accompany them. From purchasing a home and funding education to retirement planning, each milestone encapsulates a distinct facet of one's financial journey.

The establishment of financial milestones serves a dual purpose. Firstly, it provides a tangible roadmap, a series of checkpoints that guide individuals toward their overarching financial objectives. This clarity of direction enhances decision-making, enabling individuals to align their daily choices with the larger narrative of financial success.

Secondly, the act of establishing milestones becomes a source of motivation and accountability. It injects purpose into financial endeavors, transforming abstract aspirations into concrete and achievable targets. Each milestone crossed is a testament to discipline, resilience, and the ability to convert dreams into reality. This sense of accomplishment, in turn, fuels the momentum needed to tackle subsequent milestones with renewed vigor.

Moreover, financial milestones act as a dynamic framework. Life is inherently fluid, subject to changes, challenges, and unexpected opportunities. The flexibility inherent in well-established milestones accommodates these fluctuations. It allows individuals to adapt their goals in response to evolving circumstances, ensuring that the financial journey remains relevant and responsive.

In essence, "Establishing Milestones for Financial Success" is a chapter of profound intentionality—an intentional design of one's financial narrative. It transforms the nebulous concept of financial freedom into a series of achievable, measurable, and purposeful goals. Through this strategic roadmap, individuals not only chart a course towards financial success but cultivate a mindset of empowerment, resilience, and a steadfast commitment to the journey ahead.

Celebrating achievements along the journey

In the odyssey towards financial mastery, the chapter titled "Celebrating Achievements Along the Journey" becomes a vibrant interlude—a moment of reflection and exaltation amidst the ebbs and flows of the financial narrative. It underscores the importance of pausing to acknowledge the milestones, both grand and subtle, that embellish the path to financial success.

Celebration in the context of financial achievements is not a mere ceremonial act but a deliberate and integral part of the journey. It serves as a beacon, illuminating the victories, lessons, and growth amassed along the way. From the smallest triumphs, such as adhering to a budget for consecutive months, to the monumental feats of eliminating debts or achieving substantial savings goals, each accomplishment becomes a narrative thread woven into the fabric of one's financial story.

The significance of celebration lies not only in the act itself but in the profound impact it has on one's financial mindset. It acts as a psychological milestone, affirming that the journey is not solely about reaching a distant destination but about savoring the richness of the entire expedition. Celebrating achievements imbues the financial journey with positivity, reinforcing the commitment to sound financial habits and instilling a sense of fulfillment.

Moreover, celebration becomes a source of motivation and resilience. In a landscape where financial goals can sometimes seem distant or daunting, recognizing and celebrating achievements becomes a powerful tool for self-encouragement. It serves as a reminder that progress is being made, fostering a sense of momentum that propels individuals forward in the face of challenges.

The act of celebration need not be extravagant; it can be as simple as acknowledging the effort invested, sharing successes with loved ones, or treating oneself to a small indulgence. The key is the intention behind the celebration—a deliberate pause to express gratitude for the journey and to cultivate a positive outlook towards future endeavors.

Celebrating achievements along the financial journey is akin to marking waypoints on a map. It not only provides a sense of orientation, allowing individuals to reflect on how far they have come, but it also becomes a source of inspiration for the next leg of the journey. It transforms the financial narrative from a series of tasks into a dynamic and fulfilling expedition—a journey worth savoring, celebrating, and ultimately, mastering.

12.2 Continuous Growth and Learning

In the ever-evolving landscape of financial mastery, the principle of continuous growth and learning emerges as an unwavering compass—a guiding ethos that propels individuals forward on their journey toward financial success. This chapter is a testament to the dynamic nature of personal finance, emphasizing the perpetual pursuit of knowledge and the cultivation of a mindset that thrives on adaptability.

At its core, continuous growth and learning in the context of financial mastery signify an ongoing commitment to expanding one's financial literacy. It involves staying abreast of the latest trends, strategies, and tools that shape the financial landscape. From understanding investment opportunities and emerging financial technologies to navigating changes in tax regulations, the commitment to learning becomes a cornerstone for informed decision-making.

The financial journey is replete with opportunities for refinement and enhancement. This chapter encourages individuals to embrace a proactive stance, seeking out resources that deepen their understanding of complex financial concepts. Whether through books, online courses, workshops, or consultations with financial experts, the pursuit of knowledge becomes a deliberate and integral aspect of the financial journey.

Moreover, the ethos of continuous growth and learning extends beyond the technical aspects of personal finance. It encompasses the development of a holistic financial mindset—one that appreciates the interconnectedness of financial well-being with broader aspects of life. This includes cultivating skills in budgeting, financial planning, and investment strategy, as well as nurturing emotional intelligence to navigate the psychological aspects of financial decision-making.

The commitment to continuous growth also involves learning from personal experiences and adapting strategies based on real-time feedback. It encourages a reflective approach to financial decision-making, allowing individuals to glean insights from both successes and setbacks. This iterative process of learning and refinement positions individuals to make more informed and strategic choices as they progress along their financial journey.

In essence, "Continuous Growth and Learning" is not just a chapter; it is an ever-unfolding narrative that shapes the trajectory of financial success. It underscores the belief that the journey to financial mastery is not a static destination but a dynamic expedition—one that thrives on curiosity, adaptability, and a relentless pursuit of improvement. Through this commitment to continuous growth and learning, individuals not only navigate the complexities of personal finance but also cultivate a mindset that positions them as lifelong stewards of their financial well-being.

The importance of lifelong financial education

In the mosaic of personal and financial development, the significance of lifelong financial education stands as an enduring pillar—a commitment to continuous learning that transcends age, circumstance, and economic landscapes. This chapter underscores the profound impact of acquiring and applying financial knowledge throughout one's life, emphasizing that education is not a finite endeavor but a dynamic and empowering journey.

At its core, the importance of lifelong financial education lies in its ability to empower individuals with the knowledge and skills necessary to navigate the complexities of personal finance. Financial landscapes evolve, influenced by economic shifts, technological advancements, and changes in regulatory frameworks. Lifelong financial education equips individuals with the tools to understand and adapt to these dynamic forces, ensuring that they remain informed and capable stewards of their financial well-being.

Moreover, financial education serves as a powerful antidote to uncertainty. Life is rife with financial decisions, from managing day-to-day expenses to planning for major life events such as homeownership, education, and retirement. Lifelong financial education provides individuals with the foundation to make informed and strategic choices, mitigating the anxiety often associated with financial decision-making.

The commitment to ongoing financial education extends beyond the technical aspects of money management. It encompasses the cultivation of a financial mindset—one that appreciates the holistic connection between financial well-being and overall life satisfaction. Understanding the emotional and psychological dimensions of financial choices empowers individuals to make decisions aligned with their values, aspirations, and long-term goals.

In an era of rapid technological advancement, lifelong financial education also encompasses digital literacy. Understanding and leveraging financial technologies, online tools, and digital platforms become integral components of staying financially savvy in a rapidly evolving digital landscape. Lifelong learners remain agile and adaptable, harnessing the benefits of technology to optimize their financial strategies.

Furthermore, the importance of lifelong financial education is magnified in the context of generational wealth and legacy planning. It equips individuals with the foresight to create a financial legacy that extends beyond their lifetime, fostering financial well-being for future generations. Lifelong learners are not only beneficiaries of financial wisdom but become custodians of a legacy rooted in informed decision-making and strategic financial planning.

In conclusion, the importance of lifelong financial education is akin to a perennial spring—a source of nourishment, growth, and resilience. It is a commitment to continuous learning that empowers individuals to navigate the intricacies of personal finance at every stage of life. Through this commitment, individuals not only secure their financial well-being but contribute to a culture of informed decision-making, economic resilience, and enduring financial empowerment.

Staying informed and adapting to evolving financial landscapes

In the dynamic realm of personal finance, the ability to stay informed and adapt to evolving financial landscapes emerges as a cornerstone for financial well-being. This chapter underscores the imperative of remaining vigilant, proactive, and responsive to the multifaceted changes that shape the financial terrain. It is a narrative of resilience, empowerment, and the strategic prowess required to navigate the fluidity of economic climates.

At its essence, staying informed is a commitment to continuous learning—an acknowledgment that the financial landscape is not static but subject to ongoing shifts influenced by economic trends, policy changes, and technological advancements. Individuals who embrace this ethos position themselves as informed decision-makers, equipped with the insights needed to make strategic choices in alignment with their financial goals.

The journey of staying informed begins with an active engagement with financial news, trends, and developments. Whether through reputable news sources, financial publications, or digital platforms, individuals immerse themselves in a flow of information that shapes their understanding of economic dynamics. This continuous influx of knowledge serves as a compass, providing a real-time map of the financial landscape.

Furthermore, staying informed extends beyond a mere awareness of current events; it encompasses a deeper understanding of the forces that drive economic changes. This includes financial literacy—grasping concepts such as investment strategies, risk management, and the implications of policy decisions. A robust foundation of financial knowledge becomes a bulwark against uncertainty, enabling individuals to make informed choices that align with their unique financial circumstances.

Adapting to evolving financial landscapes is the natural progression of staying informed. It involves a proactive response to shifts in economic conditions, market dynamics, and regulatory environments. The ability to pivot, adjust financial strategies, and capitalize on emerging opportunities is a testament to financial agility—a quality that distinguishes those who thrive in changing landscapes.

Technological advancements play a pivotal role in the evolving financial terrain. Staying informed includes a proficiency in leveraging digital tools, financial technologies, and online resources to optimize financial decision-making. From mobile banking and investment platforms to budgeting apps and digital financial planning tools, individuals who embrace technology harness its power to enhance their financial strategies.

In conclusion, "Staying Informed and Adapting to Evolving Financial Landscapes" is not merely a chapter; it is an ongoing narrative of empowerment and adaptability. It champions the proactive pursuit of knowledge, the ability to interpret economic trends, and the agility to respond strategically to change. Through this commitment, individuals not only navigate the complexities of personal finance but become architects of their financial destinies, equipped to flourish in an ever-changing financial landscape.

Conclusion

As we draw the final chapter of "Money Mastery: Unlocking the Path to True Financial Freedom" to a close, it is not just an ending but a commencement—a transition from the pages of insight to the canvas of action. This journey has been more than a compilation of financial principles; it has been a guide to forging a profound connection with your financial destiny.

In the tapestry of financial mastery, we embarked on a holistic exploration—unveiling the intricacies of personal finance, delving into the nuances of mindset, and embracing a commitment to continuous growth. From understanding the profound impact of beliefs about money to creating a solid financial foundation, tackling debt, and navigating the realms of investment, each chapter has been a stepping stone toward true financial empowerment.

We emphasized the dynamic nature of financial landscapes and the imperative of staying informed, adaptable, and proactive. Lifelong financial education became not just a suggestion but a mandate—a commitment to cultivating knowledge that transcends generations and shapes a legacy rooted in financial wisdom.

The journey involved celebrating victories, both small and monumental, and reflecting on the profound lessons embedded in challenges. It was an exploration of not just wealth accumulation but a mindful examination of spending habits, lifestyle choices, and the alignment of financial goals with a purposeful life.

As we conclude this book, remember that financial mastery is not a destination but a perpetual expedition. It is a commitment to becoming the architect of your financial destiny, equipped with knowledge, resilience, and a mindset attuned to growth. Your journey does not end here; it transforms into a continuous loop of learning, adapting, and celebrating the milestones that pave the way to enduring financial freedom.

In the grand tapestry of life, may your financial journey be a testament to purpose, resilience, and a steadfast commitment to mastering the art of wealth creation. As you step into the chapters that follow, may you continue to unlock the full spectrum of financial freedom and, in doing so, create a life that resonates with abundance, fulfillment, and a legacy that endures beyond the pages of this book.

Here's to your journey of mastering your financial destiny—an odyssey that extends far beyond the confines of these pages and into the boundless possibilities that await.

13.1 Reflecting on Your Money Mastery Journey

As the journey of money mastery unfolds, the chapter titled "Reflecting on Your Money Mastery Journey" becomes a profound pause—an invitation to step back, contemplate, and glean insights from the financial odyssey traversed. This chapter encapsulates the transformative power of introspection, prompting individuals to assess their growth, recalibrate goals, and solidify their commitment to the principles of financial mastery.

Reflection serves as a vital compass, guiding individuals to revisit the milestones achieved, challenges surmounted, and lessons learned along the way. It is a deliberate act of self-discovery—an opportunity to uncover the intricacies of one's relationship with money, values, and aspirations. Through this introspective lens, individuals not only measure the progress made but also refine their understanding of what true financial freedom means to them.

The process of reflection is not confined to numerical achievements; it extends to the emotional and psychological dimensions of the journey. Individuals contemplate the evolution of their financial mindset, the habits cultivated, and the resilience developed in the face of financial challenges. This holistic introspection is integral to fostering a sense of gratitude for the journey and the wisdom gained through experience.

Moreover, reflecting on the money mastery journey involves a forward-looking component—a contemplation of the path ahead. It prompts individuals to refine their financial goals, align them with current life circumstances, and set new aspirations that resonate with their evolving vision of financial freedom. This anticipatory reflection becomes a blueprint for the chapters yet to unfold.

The chapter encourages individuals to celebrate not only the grand accomplishments but also the incremental victories and the perseverance exhibited during challenging times. Celebration becomes a ritual, a symbolic acknowledgment of the dedication invested in the pursuit of financial well-being. It serves as a wellspring of motivation, propelling individuals forward with renewed determination.

Reflection is not a one-time occurrence but a cyclical practice embedded in the fabric of financial mastery. Regular moments of introspection, perhaps quarterly or annually, foster a continuous loop of growth and refinement. This cyclical reflection ensures that the financial journey remains purposeful, adaptive, and attuned to the evolving landscape of life.

In essence, "Reflecting on Your Money Mastery Journey" is a chapter of profound self-discovery and intentional growth. It transforms the financial narrative from a linear progression to a dynamic and enriching expedition. Through this chapter, individuals not only assess where they stand on the spectrum of financial mastery but also lay the groundwork for a future illuminated by continued learning, adaptability, and a deep sense of fulfillment.

Encouragement and motivation for readers

Dear Reader,

As you stand at the threshold of your financial journey, know that the path ahead is brimming with potential, opportunities, and the promise of transformative growth. The pages you've just read are not merely words but an invitation—an invitation to embark on a journey of self-discovery, empowerment, and mastery over your financial destiny.

It's natural to feel a blend of excitement and perhaps a touch of trepidation as you contemplate the chapters ahead. Remember, true financial freedom is not a distant summit but a series of steps, each one bringing you closer to the life you envision. Embrace the journey, for within it lies the power to shape a future that aligns with your dreams.

In moments of challenge, recall the resilience you've cultivated. Every challenge is an opportunity to learn, adapt, and emerge stronger. You are not alone on this journey—draw inspiration from those who have faced similar paths and emerged victorious. Your potential is limitless, and your capacity for growth knows no bounds.

Celebrate your victories, no matter how small. Each step forward is a testament to your commitment and determination. As you navigate the complexities of personal finance, remember that every decision, every choice, contributes to the masterpiece of your financial story.

Embrace the concept of lifelong learning. The financial landscape is dynamic, and your knowledge is your greatest asset. Stay curious, stay informed, and let the pursuit of knowledge be a guiding light on your journey. Seize opportunities to enhance your skills, and view challenges as stepping stones to a more profound understanding of financial mastery.

Your mindset is a powerful force. Cultivate a mindset of abundance, positivity, and resilience. In moments of doubt, affirm your belief in your ability to overcome challenges and achieve your financial goals. The journey may have twists and turns, but your mindset will shape your experience.

Lastly, remember that this journey is uniquely yours. Your financial goals, aspirations, and definition of success are personal. Embrace your individuality, and let your financial journey be a reflection of your values, passions, and vision for a fulfilling life.

As you turn the page to the next chapter of your financial adventure, do so with confidence, courage, and the knowledge that you are equipped with the tools to master your financial destiny. The best chapters are yet to come, and the story you create is yours to narrate.

Here's to your journey of financial empowerment, growth, and the creation of a life that resonates with abundance and purpose. Your financial destiny awaits—embrace it with open arms.

Dear Reader,

If you've reached this page, it means you've embarked on a journey toward financial mastery within the pages of "Money Mastery: Unlocking the Path to True Financial Freedom." We sincerely hope this book has been a source of inspiration, knowledge, and practical guidance on your path to financial empowerment.

We invite you to share your thoughts and experiences by leaving a review on Kindle. Your insights can help other readers discover the transformative potential within these pages and encourage them to embark on their own journey toward financial freedom.

Here are a few prompts to consider in your review:

- **What insights did you gain?** Share specific concepts or strategies that resonated with you.
- **How has the book impacted your mindset?** Reflect on any shifts in your financial perspective or habits.
- **Were there actionable steps that made a difference in your financial journey?** Highlight practical takeaways.
- **In what ways did the book inspire you?** Whether it's a change in goals or newfound motivation, we'd love to hear about it.

Your review is not just a reflection on the book but a contribution to a community of individuals striving for financial mastery. Thank you for sharing your thoughts and being part of this journey.

Wishing you continued success on your path to financial freedom!

With gratitude,

Alex Sterling

www.ingramcontent.com/pod-product-compliance
Lightning Source LLC
Chambersburg PA
CBHW062314290526
45794CB00005B/1803